JOHN JAY, THE NATION AND THE COURT

*The Gaspar G. Bacon Lecture
on the Constitution
of the United States*

Distinguished American historian Richard B. Morris is Chairman of the History Department at Columbia University where he is Gouverneur Morris Professor. Professor Morris has taught at City College, New York, and Princeton; he was Carnegie Visiting Professor at the University of Hawaii in 1957. He has also been a member of the Institute for Advanced Study as well as Fulbright Research Scholar at the Sorbonne.

He has written and edited numerous works including *The Encyclopedia of American History* (with H. S. Commager, 1953) and *The American Revolution Reconsidered* (1967). In addition to his historical work, Professor Morris is a legal scholar and author of *Studies in the History of American Law* (1930) and *Fair Trial* (1952).

He is now serving as editor of the John Jay Papers at Columbia and preparing for publication two volumes of the first chief justice's papers. The first project to come out of the Jay Papers was Professor Morris' widely acclaimed study, *The Peacemakers,* which won the Bancroft Prize in History in 1966.

JOHN JAY
THE NATION
AND THE
COURT

Richard B. Morris

BOSTON UNIVERSITY PRESS

BOSTON, MASSACHUSETTS

1967

This book is inscribed
To the memory of
Morris Raphael Cohen
and
Felix Frankfurter

The Bacon Lectureship

The Gaspar G. Bacon Lectureship on the Constitution of the United States was established in 1927 by Mrs. Robert Bacon of New York in honor of her son, at that time Secretary of the Board of Trustees of Boston University. After several terms in the Massachusetts General Court (legislature) and two years as Lieutenant Governor, Gaspar G. Bacon retired from active politics and joined the Department of Government, College of Liberal Arts at Boston University in 1938. His teaching career was interrupted by four years of service in World War II. September 1947 found Professor Bacon back at Boston University, but only for a short period which ended suddenly with his death on Christmas Day.

Since 1927 the Bacon Lectures have been given annually by an eminent scholar or jurist in fulfillment of the terms of the deed of gift which reads, "The purpose of the Lectureship is to stimulate a study of the Constitution of the United States, its antecedents, history and doctrine, together with the results and implications thereof."

PREFACE

Almost alone among the Founding Fathers who shaped the destiny of the new nation, John Jay has not received adequate recognition for his seminal contributions as statesman and constitutional expositor. Circumstances have conspired to keep Jay out of the spotlight which has played on the other central figures of the great constitutional drama. He did not attend the Constitutional Convention. His term as first chief justice was comparatively brief. Unlike all other major figures of the time, save Franklin and Hamilton, he never became president.

Notwithstanding the secondary place often assigned to Jay, his contributions to the formation of the nation and the shaping of the Constitution entitle him to a place in the first rank of the Founding Fathers. No one who did not serve in the presidency had the opportunity to distinguish himself in as many different high state and federal offices as Jay. Save perhaps for John Quincy Adams and John Hay, no one else can claim to have been principal in the negotiation of two major treaties of the United States with foreign nations.

Historians have not dealt too charitably with Jay. They have customarily downgraded his diplomatic moves, attributing them either to unwarranted suspicion or to exorbitant vanity. Over and over they have tagged him as an antidemocratic elitist and dismissed his term on the Supreme Court as a period of marking time. Such appraisals are biased and partial. Jay's diplomatic achievements at Paris in 1782 still stand unrivalled in the annals of American diplomacy. His liberal and conciliatory posture toward more radical opponents and adherents of states-rights views, evinced in the drafting of his state's constitution in 1777 and again at the Poughkeepsie ratifying convention eleven years later, scarcely conforms to the portrait of a self-righteous and authoritarian personality. His activist role on the Supreme Court belies the image of a negative and colorless chief justice.

It has been this writer's good fortune to have been intimately associated with the work of John Jay over a considerable number of years through the massive written record of his career which has been assembled as the John Jay Papers at Columbia University. Some years ago the University Library's Special Collections acquired his papers from Jay's descendants. Both public and private papers, the collection consists of some five thousand items, exceptional both as prize autographic items and for their historical significance. The initial acquisition sparked the impulse for setting up the John Jay Papers project, which, under the writer's direction, has been engaged in searching here and abroad for Jay materials not acquired in the original purchase. In addition to further acquisitions of original manuscripts, we have located and photocopied some fifteen thousand items in private and public collections.

The John Jay Papers has been conceived as a research and selective publications project. It is planned to publish shortly two substantial volumes of highly significant but hitherto unpublished Jay Papers, with appropriate editorial apparatus, to issue a calendar of all the Jay Papers that Columbia has assembled, originals and photocopies, and to encourage the writing of monographs in the areas in which Jay had an enormous impact. The writer's recent book, *The Peacemakers,* dealing with the Great Powers and American independence, was the first publication to result from the initiation of the Jay Papers project. The interpretive essays in the present volume—the substance of the Gaspar G. Bacon Lectures on the Constitution delivered at Boston University in the fall of 1965—have drawn heavily upon the central source.

In the preparation of this book the writer has been the fortunate beneficiary of much sensible advice from Professor Herbert A. Johnson of Hunter College and Misses Mary-Jo Kline, Barbara Bennett, and Carol Berkin of Columbia University. In the preparation of copy for the printer Miss Margaret Ann Bruckner has been indispensable.

Columbia University   Richard B. Morris
March 1967

CONTENTS

I

The Wellsprings of Jay's Nationalism

I I

*Jay, the Supreme Court,
and the Subordination of the States*

I I I

*Jay, the Supreme Court,
and the Supremacy of Treaties*

Notes and Case Index

CHAPTER I

THE WELLSPRINGS
OF JAY'S NATIONALISM

John Jay stands as an embodiment of the paradoxes by which the American Revolution is especially characterized: he was a prudent revolutionary. The descriptive adjective seems antithetical. One might as well speak of a cautious volcano or a temperate tidal wave! Yet, unlike most revolutions, the War for Independence was distinguished by its concern for and emphasis upon legality. The Americans, among them John Jay, fought for the rights of Englishmen, as they believed them to be guaranteed by the British constitution, and for the rights of man as they understood them to be guaranteed by Nature and Nature's God. True, there was a seamier side to the Revolution—the tarring and feathering, lynching, and vindictive persecution of relatively inoffensive Loyalists, along with the repudiation of debts and the confiscation of Tory estates. But there was no systematic terror, no *Thermidor,* no mailed fist. From beginning to end, the Revolution was led by an elite, conservative and legal-minded. Men like Jay, trained in the law, opposed excesses and attempted to have the war fought according to rules prevailing in civilized nations. In no revolutionary leader is this legalism more evident than in the person of John Jay. Whether as chairman of the Board of Commissioners for Detecting and Defeating Conspira-

3

cies; member of the Council of Safety of his state charged with the direction of war operations (including the gathering of intelligence and the surveillance of suspected persons); chief justice of the state; president of the Congress; or a diplomat at Madrid or Paris, Jay's tight legalism and concern for justice were dominant characteristics of the man and the statesman.

A King's College graduate of the class of 1764, admitted to the New York bar four years later, Jay was associated with a group of attorneys who were acutely sensitive to the constitutional issues that were creating a rift between colonies and empire in the years immediately following the close of the French and Indian War. Even before he took up his law studies he had seen his uncle and godfather, John Chambers, place principle above office and resign his post as justice of the New York Supreme Court rather than accept a commission issued by the lieutenant governor "at the pleasure of the Crown." [1]

Jay had scarcely begun his clerkship under Benjamin Kissam when the lawyers in New York, in protest against the taking of an appeal from a jury verdict, refused en masse to represent the appellant. [2] As a law clerk Jay witnessed the lawyers' strike against the enforcement of the Stamp Act, an early instance when non-violent resistance proved an effective instrument to attain a revolutionary end. [3] The lawyer leadership of the Sons of Liberty also employed less peaceful tactics—such as street demonstrations—setting the small upcountry farmers a dangerous example. When the upcountry tenants rioted against their landowners in a leveler movement to overturn the leasehold system and obtain fee simple grants, Jay saw his fellow lawyers, tied by class and economic bonds with the landlords, support the prosecution of the tenant rioters for high treason. Jay's own mentor, Benjamin Kissam, summed up the Crown's case, although this mild-tempered patrician felt misgivings "that so many lives should be at stake upon the principles of a constructive murder." [4] Tied to the landed gentry through his mother's family, who were Van Cortlandts, it is unthinkable that Jay could have considered the bloody riots against property-owners a legitimate form of protest. At this stage of his career he preferred legal to lawless modes of redress. He defended in court the broadly based Westchester Borough franchise, an activity which brought him before the public as an attorney ready to oppose the unbridled power of the royal governor.[5]

Aside from his involvement in legal issues with political overtones, Jay was exposed during his period of law practice to the issues of federalism which, in incipient form, were cropping up within the dependent provinces of the British Empire. To take one example, on the eve of the Revolution Jay participated in a case involving the question: could a party who had recovered judgment in another province sue on a judgment in the province of New York? "A very important point," Jay commented, "and the country is much interested in its determination." Seeking a precedent within the imperial system, Jay looked into the question whether actions in England could be brought on judgments obtained in Ireland, finding "many authorities against it." [6] It might also be pointed out that the Moot, the debating society of the New York bar of which Jay was an active member, on several occasions argued the issues of interstate comity and conflict of laws between provinces.[7]

Of all the early intercolony and interstate conflicts, that over boundaries was the most persistent. In 1769 Jay served as clerk of the New York–New Jersey Boundary Commission. From the successful, if protracted settlement of that dispute Jay became familiar with the idea of a mixed commission, a device which he himself was to make use of in

5

the settlement of international disputes. Significantly, the Jay Treaty of 1794 provided for the setting up of mixed commissions to settle boundary and other claims arising from the peace of 1783, of which he was a signatory; there can be little doubt that Jay drew upon his youthful clerkship in the boundary commission in initiating this approach to the peaceful settlement of issues between nations.[8] Aside from the model suggested by the intercolony commission, Jay's protracted involvement in these tortuous negotiations impressed him with the need for some central or federal machinery to deal with conflicts between subordinate parts of the empire.

His seven years in the active practice of the law confirmed the portrait of Jay as a stickler for legal technicalities drawn by his brethren of the law. His later associates on the diplomatic front, who witnessed his tenacity on procedural points, were to corroborate that early impression. By nature conciliatory as well as cautious, Jay shocked his Tory friends when he became an out-and-out revolutionary. Exercising the prudence and restraint of the law-oriented mind, Jay had for a time resisted the drift in the Continental Congress toward independence, although he was second to none in his criticism of the harsh measures of the British ministry and Parliament. His notable "Address to the People of Great Britain," adopted by the Continental Congress on September 5, 1774, addressed itself to the constitutional issues. In lawyerlike fashion Jay asserted "that no power on earth has the right to take our property from us without our consent," claimed the right to fair trial, and denied as "heresies in English politics" the insistence of Parliament "that they have a right to bind us in all cases without exception." Why should the ministry have assumed as their own cause the minor property claims advanced by the East India Company for the tea dumped in Boston Harbor? Why should "the great council of the nation" condescend "to intermeddle with a dispute about private property?" Was this "trespass committed on some merchandise" a proper ground to suspend the charter and change the constitution of Massachusetts Bay? Appealing to the "justice" and "public spirit" of the British nation, Jay warned: "We will never submit to be hewers of wood or drawers of water for any ministry or nation in the world." [9] These were strong words, indeed, but they were a plea for the restoration of harmony and friendship, rather than a call to war. Beyond justifying the boycott of British products adopted by the Continental Congress, Jay, it should be noted, threatened no further retaliatory action. Consistent with this conciliatory stand was his role in initiating, almost a year later, the notion of the "Olive Branch Petition," and in drawing up a first draft of the document, which in final form was written by John Dickinson. [10]

Although the groundswell for independence mounted in the spring of 1776, Jay still posed as the pleader at the bar of justice, appealing to the better instincts of a monarch deceived by bad counsellors. As the pressures for a break with England mounted, Jay publicly denied that the Continental Congress aimed at independence. By now he was considered a member of the conservative faction of the congress, of which Dickinson was perhaps the chief spokesman, a faction which still favored keeping the ties to empire. [11] In the early spring of 1776 he privately expressed his disapproval of those immoderates who "observe no medium and are either all flame or all frost." [12]

The obligations of the New York Provincial Congress precluded Jay's presence at the Continental Congress when the Declaration of Independence was adopted. In any event, the New York delegation did not vote on the question on July 4 as they were awaiting instructions from their state, whose provincial congress had already adjourned. Jay himself had taken the lead in having the provincial congress hold up such instructions.[13] Whatever Jay felt about the definitive action of the Continental Congress— in which he had no direct part—he quickly took a decisive stand in putting his state solidly behind the Great Declaration. On July 9 the New York Provincial Congress adopted a set of resolutions from Jay's pen endorsing as "cogent and conclusive" the reasons assigned by congress for declaring independence. "We approve the same," he added, and pledged that we "will, at the risk of our lives and fortunes, join with the other Colonies in supporting it." [14]

The die was cast. To Jay, the congress' action was final as well as conclusive. No one henceforth was more energetic in pursuing the war to a victorious conclusion. Realistic, tenacious, and implacable, Jay, had he been "vested with absolute power" in the state, as he himself phrased it, would have laid waste the lower part of New York and shallowed the upper reaches of the Hudson to make the river impassable to British frigates. Such a move might well have prevented the British from using New York City as a base of operations as they did for seven long years.[15] Jay stressed the great importance of victory in his inspired address at the New York convention, written and adopted right before the Battle of Trenton to hearten morale impaired by the advance of Redcoat and Hessian. He declared, in words that might have come from Tom Paine's contemporary *American Crisis* pamphlet, "we do not fight for a few acres of land, but for freedom—for the freedom and happiness of millions yet unborn." Even down to the end of the war he was reconciled to continuing the fight until independence was achieved. "War must make peace for us," he told John Adams, "and we shall always find well-appointed armies to be our ablest negotiators." [16]

Accepting the inevitability of war, even though with some regret and misgivings, Jay was among the first to recognize the need for a new governmental machinery. Perhaps his initial move was prompted by a desire to counteract "that Anarchy which already too much prevails," as he expressed it.[17] But he was also motivated by a desire to improve on the provincial form of government. Like other patriots, Jay took for granted that the source of all authority was the people and that men had an indubitable right to alter, or abolish governments, and to institute new governments. But there were procedural steps to be faced. Was a revolutionary legislature empowered to frame such a constitution? Must there be a special constitutional convention? Must the charter then be submitted for ratification? Each of the several states provided its own answers to these novel questions.

When in the spring of 1776 Congress called on the states to form their own governments, Jay favored the holding of a state convention in New York to adopt such a constitution as would "continue till a peace with Great Britain may render it unnecessary." Any flickering hope was snuffed out by the Great Declaration to which John Jay almost at once pledged his adherence. Jay had indeed already expressed the opinion that the old colony government would no longer work but merely accomplish "mischief." [18]

It was this task of forming a new government that detained Jay in New York and kept him from the momentous session which adopted the Declaration of Independence. On July 6 Jay wrote Edward Rutledge: "We have a government, you know, to form; and God only knows what

9

it will resemble. Our politicians, like some guests at a feast, are perplexed and undetermined which dish to prefer." [19] The provincial congress set about the task almost at once, changing its name on July 10 to "The Convention of the Representatives of the State of New York."

That change seemed to foreclose further debate on the delicate issue of whether or not the legislature had the authority to impose a new constitution on the state without reference to the people. That spring the mechanics of New York City had contested such authority, and for a time the legislature itself was deadlocked over the issue.[20] Gouverneur Morris argued for a special constitutional convention, while John Morin Scott advocated having the legislature draft the new constitution. Jay, although on Morris' side on this question, found it expedient to back a compromise plan whereby additional members authorized to institute the new government were to be elected by the people.[21] Considering the threatening military situation, this proved to be the most practical course.

John Jay's reputation as a constitutional thinker rests in no inconsiderable part on his major role in the drafting of the first constitution of New York State, the constitution of 1777. This constitution contained some remarkable innovations in government. The authorship of that document can never be established conclusively, but it seems largely to have been the work of three men—John Jay, Robert R. Livingston, and Gouverneur Morris, with Jay playing a central role. Jay had been named to the original constitutional committee in August 1776, but his concurrent services on a secret committee to obstruct the Hudson, held up the drafting committee for a number of months. They got down to business in October, and after a number of interruptions, understandable in the light of the invasion of the state by the British forces, the constitution was drafted in its final form and submitted to the provincial congress on March 12, 1777.[22] The convention had been forced by military exigencies to move from White Plains to Harlem, then on to King's Bridge, and with the British advance up northern Manhattan, to Philipse Manor, Fishkill, Poughkeepsie, and at last across the Hudson to Kingston where the constitution was finally adopted.

One eminent constitutional authority attributes the original draft of the constitution to Jay; another the final draft. It does seem clear that the document in its final form was Jay's handiwork. Not only his own claim to authorship, but also an inspection of the debates in the convention and of Jay's correspondence serves to confirm his central role.[23]

The new government, characterized by a relatively weak governor and a strong two-chambered legislature, had certain distinctive features either innovated or adapted by John Jay. The governor shared appointing power with a council of appointment, and shared a veto power with a council of revision. A court of impeachment and correction of errors assumed functions that had traditionally been those of the legislature.

The constitution reflected Jay's outspoken support for the principle of strict separation of powers, a point of view that he was to reiterate throughout his long career in government. Originally, it seems that Jay intended to continue the colonial council as a part of the legislature, but when his draft was amended to give the governor a vote in the legislature, Jay had the proposal stricken out. Jay's thinking on the executive power reflected the critical attitude of the patriots toward the unrestrained exercise of authority by royal governors. They wanted to see that this would not happen under a republican government. What emerged from a variety of proposals to curb the governor was the Council of Appointments, clothed with large executive functions; by construction, at first practical and later by a constitutional amendment in 1801, its members were given complete control over executive appointments. This was not Jay's original intention, and as governor he later fought a bitter and losing battle with the legislature to retain a share of the appointing power. What Jay had in mind was a compromise between the governor's exclusive control over appointments and equally exclusive control by the legislature.[24] As it turned out, the members of the council in fact —and later in law—assumed complete control over executive appointments.

The germ of the notion of a council of revision—comprised of the governor, chancellor, and judges of the supreme court, and possessing a veto power to be overridden only by a two-thirds vote of the legislature—was found in the constitutional draft attributed to Jay. That draft provided that the chancellor and judges, sitting with the senate could advise and deliberate; however, Jay's proposal was modified by Robert R. Livingston and came out of committee as a council of revision in its full-dress form.

Other features of the constitution bore Jay's distinctive stamp. Conscious of his Huguenot background and the religious persecution suffered by his ancestors under the French government, Jay had a deep suspicion of Roman Catholicism. That suspicion evidenced itself in various proposals made by Jay in committee or on the floor of the convention. Thus, he proposed the section of the constitution providing for religious toleration but would have excluded Catholics from its provisions unless they publicly abjured the authority of the pope. This proposal was debated at length, and in its final form religious liberty was defined to exclude "licentiousness" or acts endangering "the safety of the state." Although unable to curb the civil rights of Catholics, Jay managed to secure the adoption of a proposal barring ministers and priests from holding civil or military office (Article 39) and to persuade his colleagues to require naturalized persons to renounce "all allegiance" to "every foreign king, prince, potentate, and state, in all matters, ecclesiastical as well as civil" (Article 42).[25]

A man of integrity, never tainted by any conflict-of-interest situation involving his private actions while a public official, Jay took a strong stand against the unethical activities of greedy land speculators. He had a provision inserted in the constitution invalidating purchases or contracts for the sale of lands from the Indians after October 14, 1775. Fearing corrupt bargains, collusion, and nepotism, Jay was especially insistent that judges not have the power to appoint the clerk of court. To withhold appointing power from the judges would, as Jay expressed it, "avoid that odium to which that part of the Constitution will now be exposed, viz., that it was framed by lawyers, and done with design to favour the profession." He also insisted that the Supreme Court was the "most competent" body to determine the qualifications of the attorneys who practiced before it as well as before the inferior courts and therefore should have exclusive jurisdiction over admission to the bar.[26] His insistence undoubtedly prevented the creation of a divided legal profession; with one group, like the solicitors of England, practicing before the lower courts, and another, like the British barristers, having a monopoly of practice in the higher courts.

Although historians have consistently portrayed Jay as a high Federalist unsympathetic to democracy, the record hardly supports this characterization. Elitist though he was, Jay recognized how essential popular participation was to the stability of republican government. In drafting the state constitution, Jay originally proposed that the franchise

be open to all who had paid both state and county taxes—
a proposal very close to universal manhood suffrage in that
day. The committee later restricted the vote to owners or
lessees of real property. This restriction would have dis-
qualified a good many freemen in Albany and New York
City who, since 1691, had been entitled to vote for members of the assembly. To avoid disfranchising those who
were not owners or lessees of real property in those two
cities, Jay put through an amendment which preserved the
right of suffrage to persons who were then freemen in
Albany or who had become freemen in New York on or
before October 14, 1775.[27] He thus struck a strong blow
in the battle for liberalization of the franchise. Jay also
succeeded during the debates in having voting by ballot
substituted for the viva-voce method of electing representatives, although he had the detailed procedure for balloting
stricken out. His draft had also provided means whereby
illiterate voters could indicate their choice, but the Convention was not prepared to go that far. All in all, Jay's
constitutional innovations, motions, and amendments
hardly support the anti-democratic label that historians
have attached to his name.

One of Jay's most significant efforts was his endeavor
to have a clause inserted in the constitution of 1777 forbidding the continuation of slavery. He held the institu-
tion of slavery in abhorrence; he was to become a president
of the New York Manumission Society in the postwar
period, and his sons were later renowned leaders of the
antislavery movement and worked in close collaboration
with William Lloyd Garrison. In the light of his lifetime
aversion to slavery, it was fitting and proper that during
Jay's term as governor of New York he was to affix his
signature to a bill providing for the end of slavery in the
state. It is also interesting to note Jay's farsighted vision in

advocating the inclusion in the constitution of a section for "the support and encouragement of literature." His ideas were too advanced for his day; a similar rebuff was meted out to John Quincy Adams when as president he made a similar proposal. Not until the Kennedy–Johnson era, has the national government moved into areas which Washington, Jay, and John Quincy Adams long ago felt to be its proper sphere.

Although Jay regarded the birth of the state constitution as "premature" and has been charged by some with dilatory tactics, he vowed to do all in his "power to nurse and keep it alive." As Jay put it to his colleagues, Robert R. Livingston and Gouverneur Morris, he was "far from approving the Spartan law which encouraged parents to destroy such of their children as perhaps by some gross accident might come into the world misshapen." [28] Even so, Jay was by no means uncritical of the constitution of 1777, so largely his own brainchild. Later as governor of New York he had the dubious satisfaction of finding the restraints it imposed on the executive authority too severe and impractical and in need of revision.

Jay rejected an invitation to be a candidate for the governorship in 1777, despite the financial attractions of the office; he preferred instead to remain in the post of chief justice to which he had only just been named and in which he felt he could "be more useful to the State." [29] Jay hoped that the government would "be committed to proper Hands," lest it be "weak and unstable at home, and contemptible abroad." General Schuyler was Jay's own choice, and his instinct was sound. [30] Schuyler might well have been more effective as an executive than in a military capacity, where he hardly shone. Schuyler was not elected, however, and George Clinton, who assumed the executive post, proved in time to be an enemy of the national principles to which Jay was dedicated. At least Jay could take satisfaction in the fact that "our Constitution is universally approved, even in New England, where few New York productions have credit."

Jay did not permit his reservations about a constitution, which in large part he had written, to influence his strong backing of the state's new charter of government. In a charge to the grand jury in the spring of 1777, delivered after he had assumed the chief justiceship of the state's Supreme Court, he declared: "Whoever compares our present with our former Constitution will find abundant reason to rejoice in the exchange, and readily admit that all the calamities incident to this war will be amply compensated by the many blessings flowing from this glorious revolution." [31] In singling out the more distinctive and commendable aspects of the state constitution, Jay adverted "to those great and equal rights of human nature, which should forever remain inviolate in every society"—including liberty of conscience and the equal protection of the laws—and to the organization of the three branches of the government so "as to promise permanence to the constitution, and give energy and impartiality to the distribution of justice."

One cannot leave the period of Jay's chief justiceship of the state during the early years of the Revolution without mentioning one case which illustrates his meticulous regard for procedural regularity. On October 1, 1777, his court was presented with a petition for a writ of habeas corpus from one Thomas Hadden, then confined in the Ulster county jail. Jay denied the writ on the ground that under an act of the state legislature the court officers appointed by the constitutional convention were to be approved by the Council of Appointment at its first session. As the council had held a session and had failed to act on the appointment of the judges, he found no course other than to deny the writ. When the issue came up on petition to the assembly, that body upheld the court and requested the Council of Appointment to approve the slate of judges which had been sent down to it. Such action was taken by the Council on October 17.[32] When some years later the British government sought to enter into diplomatic negotiations with Jay as an American peace commissioner, it found him similarly adamant about concluding a preliminary treaty without a formal exchange of powers between the principals. Jay the lawyer, who made recognition of the United States a precondition to any treaty, was always a stickler for protocol.[33]

Jay's services on behalf of his state and nation in the early years of the Revolution constituted his apprenticeship as a nationalist statesman. His experiences in those years as an architect of the first New York state constitution, as chief justice of his own state, and as president of the Continental Congress in the year 1779, all helped mold his nationalist outlook. It was Spain, however, where Jay served as unacknowledged American commissioner, that was to mark the turning point in his nationalist thinking. His frigid reception at the Spanish court could not have failed to affect him, as it had John Adams, who was experiencing problems of his own in dealing with the French foreign office. "There is something in the European understanding different from those we have been used to," Adams remarked at this time. Referring to the Conde de Floridablanca, Spain's first minister, he remarked that men "of the greatest abilities, and the most experience, are with great difficulty brought to see, what appears to us, as clear as day. It is habit, it is education, prejudice, what you will, but so it is." [34] With a shrewdness and realism surpassing that of the Continental Congress, Jay proffered the Spaniards the relinquishment of America's claim to the Mississippi, but prudently placed a limited duration on the offer, making it conditional upon Spain's promptly recognizing American independence and entering into an alliance with her. Suffering an intense myopia on the American question, Floridablanca signally failed to snatch advantages for Spain while they still could be had for the asking. Finally writing off both Spanish aid and recognition, Jay predicted, in a letter to Franklin, that the time would come, when a "just, a free, and brave people" will have "nothing to fear" from the Spaniards, and nothing "to request of them." [35]

Appointed a commissioner to negotiate the peace in Paris, Jay protested the instructions which bound the American commissioners to the French court. Fearing—and we must now say on the basis of a full-dress review of the evidence, with good reason—that France favored splitting the territory west of the Appalachians between Spain and Britain, Jay took the controversial step of sending his own emissary to Lord Shelburne at the latter's secluded Wiltshire estate, Bowood. He did so without consulting Benjamin Franklin, whose pro-French sympathies he distrusted. The result was a quick decision by the British government to adopt an acceptable formula for recognizing America independence, the major obstacle to a preliminary peace. The peace negotiations brought into the open the divergence between the nationalist objectives of America and the war goals of the European coalition against England. In their quest for a durable peace for a new nation under a republican government, Jay and his associates in Paris were setting the mood of a revolutionary age, while France and Spain, in their efforts to retrieve influence and properties they had hitherto been forced to surrender, were casting backward glances toward a time that would never return. Nevertheless, as *The Peacemakers* reminds us, the peace negotiations began as an encounter between innocence and guile; but the Americans rapidly acquired a measure of sophistication sufficient for the task at hand. Neophytes in the art of secret diplomacy at the start, Jay and his colleagues were the peers of their Old World counterparts at the finish. "Undisciplined marines as we were," Adams commented, "we were better tacticians than was imagined." [36]

From his vantage point in Europe Jay looked across the broad ocean to the American states and was appalled that with victory came intrigue and dissension. In August 1782, at the height of the preliminary peace negotiations, he wrote a New York legal associate:

> Every good American will zealously endeavor to remove all ground of future dissension between the States. Our power, respectability, and happiness will forever depend on our Union. Many foreign nations would rejoice to see us split to pieces because we should then cease to be formidable and such an event would afford a fine field for their intrigues. Let us keep peace among ourselves, for whenever the members quarrel the whole body must suffer.[37]

In the spring of the following year, Jay wrote Washington that both ally and erstwhile foe would view the increasing power of America with serious concern and would "secretly endeavour to foment divisions among us." Therefore, he advised, let us settle our boundaries expeditiously and remove other grounds of such dissension that impair harmony and union.[38] Again in the mid-summer of 1783 he complained to his father-in-law, Governor William Livingston of New Jersey, about the reluctance of the states to pay "necessary taxes." Their conduct, he pointed out, injured "both their reputation and interest abroad as well as at home, and tends to cherish the hopes and speculations of those who wish we may become and remain an unimportant divided people." Every event that would retard the rising power of America would be agreeable to European nations, he pointed out. Their jealousies made it clear that "a continental national spirit should therefore pervade our country—and Congress should be enabled by a grant of the necessary powers, to regulate the commerce and general concerns of the Confederacy, and we should remember that to be constantly prepared for war is the only way to have peace." [39] Robert Morris and Hamilton were quite independently saying much the same thing at this time.

Europe waited impatiently for America to fall apart. The new nation could be expected to share the lethargy of other republics, a lethargy compounded by sectional rivalries, a French foreign office memorandum to the Spaniards pointed out by way of consolation. In downgrading the durable character of the American Republic, Vergennes by no means stood alone among the statesmen of Europe; Baron von der Goltz, the Prussian ambassador at Paris, saw in America "only a people poor, exhausted, and afflicted with the vices of corrupt nations." His monarch, the great Frederick, predicted that "little by little, colony by colony, province by province," the Americans would "rejoin England and their former footing." [40]

If men of little vision and less faith could not discern the shape of things to come, patriots like Jay possessed a prescience which had rendered their diplomacy at once effectual and, by the same token, very distasteful to their European counterparts. Jay recognized that, aside from the military dangers posed to the new American nation by the presence of British and Spanish neighbors in North America, the prospect of an unremitting trade war constituted an equally formidable threat. John Jay as a peace commissioner had tirelessly sought to have a reciprocal trade clause inserted in the peace treaty with Great Britain. In this effort he had the support of Richard Oswald, the British peace plenipotentiary, and of Lord Shelburne, who in many matters was a statesman with a vision far ahead of his time. But the North–Fox ministry that succeeded Shelburne yielded to the opposition of the shippers and mercantilists, and the concept of trade on a reciprocal basis with America died stillborn. When in July 1783, the British inaugurated their restrictive trade policy, Jay pronounced it "impolitic as well as ill timed." In the long run Britain would suffer, not America, provided that America enacted a navigation act based on the principle of reciprocity.[41] But to do so required a stronger framework of government than the weakly structured Articles of Confederation.

While John Jay was also concerned with army mutinies, boundary disputes, and other feuds threatening the internal union of the Confederation, he kept his eye on what Julian P. Boyd has quite correctly called "the gravest threats to the existence of the United States." These were external in origin, and were epitomized by British dumping and trade monopoly. The reframing of British mercantilist policy in those years immediately following the peace of 1783 may well have contributed more to the convocation of the Constitutional Convention of 1787 and to its success, Dr. Boyd suggests, "than many who sat in that august body," a view which this writer must endorse.[42]

Jay was merely one among a number of Federalist worthies who were in general agreement about the weakness of the Confederation. They attributed the weakness to a variety of factors—financial muddling by the states; English dumping of trade goods; the loss of the British West Indian market; paper money; stay laws; state tariffs; but, above all, to the lack of coercive power by a central authority. As an observer in charge of foreign affairs, Jay shared the view of his correspondent John Adams, then minister to the

Court of Saint James, that the conduct of foreign affairs was the most critical link in the American system of government. "I may reason till I die to no purpose," declared Adams in June 1785. "It is unanimity in America, in measures, which shall confute the British sophisms and make them feel, which will ever produce a fair treaty of commerce." [43]

Jay's strong national views were perhaps most cogently set forth during his occupancy of the office of secretary for foreign affairs in his criticism of the consular convention with France. Jay considered the draft originally agreed upon by the Comte de Vergennes and Benjamin Franklin to be incompatible with American sovereignty. One of his numerous objections to the draft convention arose from the provision that French consuls were required to present their commissions on arrival *in the respective states*. Vergennes had therein expressed a well-justified caution in dealing with a federal government which had no power over the commerce of the several states. The original draft also allowed the consuls extraterritorial jurisdiction in both civil and criminal cases between their own nationals residing in the territory of the other party; in cases between a French subject and an American citizen, the domestic tribunals were to have cognizance. Jay resented all suggestion of extraterritorial justice and had previously opposed the extradition for trial of a Frenchman guilty of an assault upon the French consul general in America, Barbé-Marbois.[44] In addition, Jay opposed a provision in the convention authorizing consuls not only to arrest and sequester ships of the subjects of his nation, but also to send them back, and to do the same with captains, masters, sailors, or *passengers*. By these provisions one party to the convention, France, was enabled to exercise an effective restraint on emigration and to prevent the nationalization of any of its subjects within the domains of the United States. The lack of true reciprocity was also seen in one provision giving full and complete immunity for the persons, houses, and papers of consuls without making them specifically amenable to the laws of the land, as Jay preferred;[45] another, likewise unacceptable provision, would allow consuls to appoint agents with consular privileges and immunities to serve in distant parts of the country. He rightly recognized that such agents would be engaged quite as much in obtaining political and military intelligence as in expediting commercial transactions. No similar privilege was conceded to the Americans by the convention, which restricted American consuls to French European ports.

Jay's case against the convention has been deemed "impregnable" by a foremost scholar of the period, and brought about an extensive revision of the consular convention.[46] A second convention was negotiated by the Comte de Vergennes and Thomas Jefferson, who had succeeded Franklin as minister to France. This convention omitted the obnoxious features controlling emigration and nationality, allowed consular agents to engage in restricted mercantile operations, but without enjoying consular immunities; and provided for delivery of commissions to the federal government instead of the states. Jay was not too content with this convention either, for it still conferred consular jurisdiction over French nationals. Nonetheless, he advised its ratification. The 1788 consular convention with France became the first treaty ever to receive the formal sanction of the Senate of the United States.

Jay's special handling of the problem posed by the Barbary pirates casts a shaft of light on how his nationalistic views and objectives governed his conduct of diplomacy. Before the Revolution, American ships plying the Mediterranean had been protected by the British navy from piratical attacks emanating from the Barbary states. With independence, this protection was withdrawn, and in fact the British, as well as other European powers, found it was in their interest *not* to protect American ships and, in effect, to keep them out of the Mediterranean trade. Although a treaty was negotiated with Morocco in 1786–1787, eliminating the problem with that power, the other North African states—Algiers, Tunis, and Tripoli—proved less amenable. By 1788, twenty-one American citizens were enslaved in the pirate ports of those states, with Algiers the most notorious malefactor. Jay agreed with Adams and Jefferson that the best way to deal with the Barbary powers was at the cannon's mouth, but the new nation was not prepared to retaliate as Congress was unable to maintain a navy. Instead, Congress advised Jay to buy a treaty, a common practice in those days. Jay objected. He pointed out that it was impossible to raise money for such a loan and suggested instead that the most immediately practical approach would be for the states directly interested to ransom their citizens. He made this proposal with tongue in cheek no doubt, but in the confident expectation that this gruesome example of abject surrender would bring home to all the necessity of a stronger government and thus hasten the initiation of needed reforms in the Confederation. "This war does not strike me as a great evil," he wrote the president of Congress in 1785. "The more we are ill-treated abroad the more we shall unite and consolidate at home." For this reason, too, among others, he opposed joining a confederation of European powers to put down the pirates.[47]

To Samuel Flagg Bemis, Jay's policy, "cold-blooded as it seems, appears to have been advisable . . . Only when a Federal government strong enough to command the respect of foreign nations could be created, would there be any hope of stopping the outrageous operations of these barbarous pirate princes." [48]

By the end of the confederation period Jay's policies and conduct in office, as well as his utterances both public and private, had stamped him as a strong nationalist with positive views on reforming the Confederation's charter of government. The need for a separation of powers and a system of checks and balances were constant themes running through Jay's letters. "I have long thought," he wrote Jefferson in 1786, "and become daily more convinced, that the construction of our Federal government is fundamentally wrong. To vest legislative, judicial and executive powers in one and the same body of men, and that, too, in a body daily changing its members, can never be wise. In my opinion, those three great departments of sovereignty should be forever separated, and so distributed as to serve as checks on each other." [49] Again: "Let Congress legislate," he wrote Washington in 1787. "Let others execute. Let others judge." Then he asked the crucial question revealing his basically republican leanings: "Shall we have a King? Not in my opinion, while other experiments remain untried." In that same letter he advocated a chief executive possessing a veto over the acts of a dual-chambered congress—the upper house appointed for life, the latter annually. Here perhaps were the seeds of Hamilton's plan presented to the federal convention only six months later. How about democracy? Must that be safeguarded, too? Not perhaps to the same degree as the republican system, for, as Jay expressed it to Washington, "Our government should in some degree be suited to our manners and circumstances, and they, you know, are not strictly democratical." [50]

Indeed, of all the high Federalists save perhaps Hamilton, Jay held the most advanced views on centralization and the subordination of the states. He wrote John Lovell in 1785: "It is my first wish to see the United States assume and merit the character of one great nation, whose territory is divided into different States merely for more convenient government and the more easy and prompt administration of justice, just as our several States are divided into counties and townships for the like purposes." [51] Jay's rather startling observation proved an apt forecast of issues to come up before the Supreme Court.

When Shays' Rebellion erupted in western Massachusetts the Founding Fathers mostly took a serious view of the affair. "We are fast verging to anarchy and confusion," Washington wrote James Madison on November 5, 1786. Jay likewise regarded the insurrection as posing a threat to the general security. Writing to Edward Rutledge the following month, he remarked, "I cannot persuade myself that the conciliatory measures of government will produce tranquillity. Justice must have a sword as well as a balance." [52] On the very same day he wrote to George Read hitherto unpublished comments on the uprising:

The Recess (if I may so call it) of Congress gives their officers too much leisure at present; and there is Reason to fear that the Members will be as long in convening this Year, as they were last. Business is at a Stand for Want of an adequate Representation. The Langour of the States is to be lamented—many Inconveniences have already arisen from it, and if continued, serious Evils will awaken our People. Our Affairs my dear Sir are in a delicate Situation, and it is much to be wished that the real Patriots throughout the States would exert themselves to render it more safe and respectable. The Feuds in Massachusetts are rather suspended than extinguished. What Events they may produce is uncertain, but I should not be surprized, if much Trouble was to result from them. The public Creditors will soon become importunate, and Congress cannot create the Means of satisfying them. It is true that Order usually succeeds Confusion—but it is a high price to pay for order; especially when a little virtue and good Sense would procure it for us on very reasonable Terms. If the best Men could be prevailed upon to come forward and take the Lead in our Legislatures as well as in Congress, and would unite their Endeavours to rescue their Country from its present Condition, our affairs both at Home and abroad, would soon wear a more pleasing aspect. It is Time for our people to distinguish more accurately than they seem to do, between Liberty and Licentiousness. The late Revolution would lose much of its Glory as well as Utility, if our Conduct should confirm the Tory Maxim, that "Men are incapable of governing themselves." [53]

Not long thereafter Jay observed: "What may be the issue of those disturbances, or how far they will extend, is as yet far from certain." What was certain and manifest, however, was "the inefficiency of the Federal government," and Jay wrote his correspondent in Spain: "How it is to be amended is a question that engages the serious attention of the best people in all the States." [54] Our situation calls for "exertion" not "reflection," Jay wrote Washington on the same day.

Jay was among the first to foresee the consequences of the Confederation government's lack of authority. Writing to French banker Ferdinand Grand in December 1785, he pointed out that the necessity of conferring such authority was becoming "more and more evident" and ventured the prediction "that the people will daily become more and more inclined to confer it." [55] Thus the convention proposed by Virginia might "do some good," he wrote Washington in March of 1786; he contributed his mite to the federal lobby with the observation: "An opinion begins to prevail that a general Convention for revising the Articles of Confederation would be expedient." With considerable prescience he added: "Whether the people are yet ripe for such a measure, or whether the system proposed to be attained by it, is only to be expected from calamity and commotion, is difficult to ascertain." But the plan was already being concerted for "a general Convention," and Jay was obviously in on it.[56]

In its conduct of foreign affairs, the weakness of the Congress of the Confederation was perhaps more evident than in any other field. Said Jay in July 1787: "So much have other concerns employed the time of Congress in ordinary, and so seldom has it been in their power to take up business that required the presence of nine states, that I have long found myself in an awkward situation: anxious to despatch the affairs of the Department, and yet unable to proceed from want of the directions of Congress." [57]

Jay's strong Federalist views prevented his being named a delegate to the Constitutional Convention. Despite the fact that as secretary for foreign affairs he occupied the highest executive post in the land, he was, like everyone else, kept in the dark about what was going on in the Convention, which strictly observed the rule of secrecy.[58] The suspense was fortunately not protracted, for the Convention sat only four months. Displaying commendable vigor and determination and an extraordinary ability to obtain a consensus, despite several crucial differences among the delegates, the federal convention submitted to the nation an entirely new constitution of government, completely scrapping the Articles.

With the disclosure of the Constitution's text, Jay quickly became a leading champion of ratification. With Hamilton and Madison he collaborated on the famous *Federalist* letters, writing numbers two through five and sixty-four. He would indubitably have done much more, but between the fall of 1787, when the fifth *Federalist* letter appeared, and March 7, 1788, the date of publication of No. 64, the next and last contribution of John Jay to that great seminal work of constitutional thought, Jay suffered serious ill health. He seems for a time to have been painfully crippled by arthritis, from which he had not completely recovered even in late February of 1788. That recovery, it might be added, was seriously jeopardized by an unfortunate accident. On a Monday afternoon in mid-April, Jay and General Clarkson came to the rescue of a group of city doctors who had taken refuge in the New York city jail to protect themselves from a mob objecting to the allegedly sacrilegious autopsy activities of the medical profession. When Jay reached the jail, near the present site of City Hall, he was struck on the forehead by a stone and fell inert.[59] For a time it was thought that he had suffered permanent brain injury, but he evidently recovered some time that spring when the public first read his notable *Address to the People of New York,* a pamphlet which ranks with the *Federalist* letters as among the most notable contributions of the pro-Constitution camp to the ratification movement.

From his five *Federalist* letters, his address, and his major role in the debates in the New York ratifying convention, Jay's ideas about the Constitution clearly emerge.

Jay's first contribution to the *Federalist* series was published on October 31, 1787, four days after Hamilton's initial essay.[60] He at once addressed himself to the argument propagated by those antifederalists who maintained that safety and happiness should be sought not in union, but in a division of the states into distinct confederacies or sovereignties. Pointing out the geographical advantages which served to unite the thirteen states, he also adverted to the common language, religion, customs, and attachment to the same principles of government for which they had fought side by side through a long and bloody war. "This country and this people," Jay remarked in an eloquent passage, "seem to have been made for each other, and it appears as if it was the design of Providence, that an inheritance so proper and convenient for a band of brethren, united to each other by the strongest ties, should never be split into a number of unsocial, jealous and alien sovereignties." He warned that those who wanted to substitute a number of distinct confederacies for the plan for ratification proposed by the Convention were jeopardizing the continuance of the union; he closed with these words: "Whenever the dissolution of the Union arrives, America will have reason to exclaim in the words of the Poet, 'FAREWELL, A LONG FAREWELL, TO ALL MY GREATNESS.'"

In the third *Federalist* essay, Jay contended that a disunited America was more likely to be provocative of war than a united country; military security would come from a perpetuation and strengthening of the Union. The treaties the Americans had made and would make in the future were more likely to be punctually observed by one national government than by thirteen separate states or by three or four distinct confederacies. Jay praised the wisdom of the Convention in committing questions in adjudication under treaties to the federal judiciary instead of to a "variety of independent courts and judges appointed by different and independent Governments."

In considering the possibility of war resulting from aggression, Jay took occasion to point out that "not a single Indian war" had been provoked by the federal government, but that on several occasions Indian hostilities were aroused "by the improper conduct of individual states." He warned that states bordering on the Spanish and British territories would, "under the impulse of sudden irritation, and a quick sense of apparent interest or injury, "be the most likely to excite war by direct violence"; his words were indeed prophetic.

Jay, in the fourth *Federalist* paper, followed up his analysis of the problems of military security with a discussion of the comparative commercial prospects under the Articles of Confederation and the Constitution. He reminded his readers that the Americans were the rivals of the French and the British in the fisheries and of most European nations in the carrying trade. He pointed out the extent to which America placed in jeopardy the trade monopolies that certain European powers sought to maintain in their commerce with China and India. To maintain such monopolies, he noted, Spain continued to shut the Mississippi to American navigation, and Britain excluded Americans from the St. Lawrence. All of these sources of friction could readily prompt a jealous foreign government to find a pretext for war; but confronted by a united American government, a foreign power might have second thoughts about pursuing a belligerent course. Jay also alluded to the disadvantage of having separate armies and navies run by the thirteen states, and to the dangers of nonsupport or neutrality by some states in the event that one or several states were attacked. The behavior of foreign nations toward us would be in large measure determined by the image of America held abroad. If we seemed united, foreign powers would be more disposed to cultivate our friendship than to provoke our resentment.

In the fifth *Federalist* Jay drew upon the example of the small island of England broken up and divided for centuries into three nations. Should the United States likewise be divided into three or four confederacies, the most northern would probably soon prove the most formidable. The result would be jealousies and animosities, which would render untenable the notion that stable military combinations among the three or four states could be created. Remember, Jay warned, these three or four confederacies would be *"distinct nations,"* and as such would be more worried about conquest from each other than from abroad and more likely to make alliances with foreign nations than between themselves.

Considered the outstanding expert on foreign affairs, Jay was assigned the task of discussing the role of the Senate in the making of treaties. This he treated in the sixty-fourth *Federalist,* the original draft of which, in a form considerably different from the published one, is among the items uncovered by the Jay Papers project. Jay assumed that senators, by virtue of their indirect popular election through the state legislatures, would necessarily be men of commanding eminence and judgment, and along with the president, the men "who best understand our national interests." In the negotiation of treaties, he reminded his readers, secrecy and dispatch were sometimes requisite. Since the secrecy of a body like the Senate could not be relied upon, the framers of the Constitution conferred the power of making treaties upon the president, who must act nonetheless with the senators' advice and consent. At the same time, there are occasions when treaties must be negotiated with dispatch, and only the president is in a position to discern and profit by "these tides in national affairs." Refuting the fallacious notion that treaties should be repealable at pleasure, he reminded his readers that a treaty was a bargain and that it would be impossible to find a nation that would make any bargain with us which would bind them absolutely but obligate us only so long and so far as we might think proper to be bound by it. He declared that the notion that the president and two-thirds of the Senate would ever be susceptible to corruption was "too gross and too invidious to be entertained." [61] Granted such an unthinkable situation should arise, however, a treaty obtained by fraud would, like other fraudulent contracts, be "null and void by the law of nations," while the culprits would be subject to the impeachment procedure set forth in the Constitution.

Most powerful of all Jay's polemics on behalf of the Constitution was his notable pamphlet, *An Address to the People of the State of New York*. Written during the winter of 1788 and published that spring, it refuted point by point the ill-tempered criticisms of the Constitution and its framers which were then being given currency. Signed "A Citizen of New York," the pseudonym was quickly penetrated, and Franklin suggested that the cause of ratification would be aided if Jay would publicly accept credit for authorship.[62] No more trenchant and irrefutable criticism of the weaknesses of the Confederation had been written at the time, and it is curious that those who have attributed the notion that there was a "critical period" to a conspiracy of the Founding Fathers have ignored the authority and reasoning of this address. Jay praised the American union formed under peril as "the child of wisdom," blessed by heaven, and responsible for "our political salvation." With the coming of peace a sense of security had loosened the bonds of union. Jay found that "the spirit of private gain expelled the spirit of public good."

Jay criticized the government of the Confederation as "destitute of power, and so constructed as to be very unfit to be trusted with it." He indicted the Confederation for its two major weaknesses—Congress' lack of power to raise money to maintain an army or to enforce the terms of peace and its lack of power to enforce the regulation of commerce. What was the result? "Almost every national object of every kind is at this day unprovided for," he charged. The economic scene was deplorable. He cited the loss of the fur trade to Canada, the decline of shipyards and the American carrying trade, the barring of foreign markets to the United

States, the rise of debt, the alarming increase of farm fore-closures. Jay shrewdly pointed out that the antifederalists' proposal for a new convention would have far less chance of reaching a consensus than the old one had, because of the divisive effect of the Federalist and Antifederalist parties, now fully emergent but nonexistent when the old convention met.[63]

All of Jay's contributions had been published before the New York state ratifying convention began its crucial deliberations. Jay quickly became one of the three undisputed leaders of the pro-Constitution party, along with Hamilton and Robert R. Livingston. He did not regard the Constitution as a counsel of perfection, but as he wrote to Washington in midwinter of 1788, "it establishes some great points, and smooths the way for a system more adequate to our national objects." In that same letter, whether by coincidence or not, he adverted to the advantages of breeding mules in the country, and pointed out the difficulty of obtaining good male asses. By the time Washington's reply reached Jay, the debate in the press over ratification had reached frenzied proportions. Indeed, so formidable was the opposition in New York state that, in Jay's view, "the issue appears as problematical." Perhaps it was fortuitous but in his original draft letter in reply to Washington Jay observed: "To say that we have no asses in this State would be saying too much. I wish we could exchange a few of them for Jacks and Jennies. We might then obtain a much more valuable race of mules than those we now have."[64]

As the moment for assembling the state convention approached, Jay informed Washington that the majority of the convention would be "composed of antifederal characters." Then he made a bold prediction. "It is doubtful," he said, "whether the leaders will be able to govern the party." The leaders wanted to reject the Constitution with "as little debate and as much speed as may be." [65] If that was their strategy, the Federalist spokesmen quickly scotched it. They were prepared to debate the Constitution provision by provision if it took all summer—and they had one or two aces up their sleeve. First, was the fact that the momentum for adoption among other states was well under way. The issue was still in contest in Virginia and New Hampshire, but once nine states had ratified the Constitution, the new government would be in being, and New York's position would be anomalous. Secondly, Jay and other leaders sedulously passed the word that if the antifederalists were obstructive, the southern part of the state would seek to separate from the northern and adhere to the union—a dreadful notion, for what remained of the state would be a landlocked republic. [66] Offstage Jay kept harping on that possibility, and the prospect, as he reported to Washington, "operates powerfully on the minds of the opposite party," while at the same time "the Constitution constantly gains advocates among the People." [67]

The oratorical laurels at the Poughkeepsie convention have been traditionally awarded to Alexander Hamilton; but whatever votes Hamilton may have gained by his debating skills were nullified by the patronizing, and even arrogant, tone that overlaid his arguments. The antifederalists feared Hamilton as much as they suspected his conversion to republicanism. In contrast to Hamilton, Jay couched his arguments in more palatable dress. His temper always under control, Jay was invariably agreeable and conciliatory to his opponents and was universally trusted. From contemporary evidence Jay's activities both on and off the floor of the convention proved more consequential than those of any other Federalist in winning over the "antis" to the cause of unconditional ratification. [68] In the debates, Jay upheld the constitutional provision on the size of the representation in Congress and supported granting to Congress the right to prescribe the time, place, and manner of holding elections.[69] It was the national government, he felt, which could best express the will of the people on this issue and could give them assurance that where the states by design or accident neglected to appoint representatives "there should be some constitutional remedy for this evil." He further advocated conferring upon the federal government the power to levy direct taxes. In support of the last point, he asserted that "a government which was to accomplish national purposes should command the national resources." [70] Running through all his arguments is the theme that a strong, energetic federal government must have enough power to "provide for the general interests of the United States." What in fact he was prepared to underwrite was a broadly based taxing authority for the federal government. Jay argued against a motion to curb the borrowing power of Congress; the mover had expatiated on the dangers of corruption in the national government, but Jay once again pointed to the separation of powers and checks and balances to provide assurance against such corruption.[71]

If the eloquence and reasoned arguments of the Federalist leaders were not enough, the threat to secede from the northern section of the state carried additional weight; one by one the opposition was worn down. Finally the issue narrowed to whether the Constitution would be ratified *conditionally,* subject to the adoption of certain amendments, or *unconditionally,* but with amendments recommended for consideration and adoption. On July 11 Jay moved the unconditional ratification of the Constitution and from then on assumed the uncontested floor leadership of the Federalists in debates against ratifying the Constitution conditionally. Largely through his efforts a compromise was finally reached whereby the convention resolved unanimously to prepare a circular letter to the state legislatures recommending a general convention to consider amendments.[72]

It bespeaks the confidence that a sharply divided convention held in John Jay that his draft of the circular letter, with trivial amendments, was the one adopted.[73] The draft strongly urged amendments, and the calling of a convention "to meet at a period not far remote." Indubitably, Jay was content that no such convention was ever held, since Congress obviated the need for such a meeting by quickly adopting the Bill of Rights which the state legislatures just as expeditiously ratified.

A patrician with a revolutionary past, committed to the ideals of a republic in which the people, directed by a virtuous and educated elite, would govern, and to a national government with power to act, Jay was unlike the conservatives of the present day who wish to return to a past that can never be recaptured. His call for the establishment of a strong national government and for the creation of a new kind of republican federalism constituted a sharp break with the political ways of the past, to which his opponents, the diehard states' rights particularists, wished to adhere. In view of later history, of a terrible Civil War fought over an outmoded issue of states' rights, and the more recent emergence of a welfare state, possessed with broad powers to maintain economic stability and national security, Jay now emerges as a forward-looking thinker, one who did not stand in fear of change. Much as he deplored the violence of the French Revolution, much as he recognized the venal influences which can sway and even corrupt the multitude, and despite the demagogic attacks upon his character by the populace at the time of the Jay Treaty, he did not lose faith in the virtue of that revolution to which he had committed his life, his fortune, and his sacred honor. As late as 1810 he wrote to his English friend, the abolitionist William Wilberforce: "The French Revolution has so discredited democracy, and it has so few influential advocates in Europe, that I doubt its giving you much more trouble. On the contrary, there seems to be a danger of its depreciating too much. Without a portion of it there can be no free government." [74]

By the year 1810, Jay, the retired statesman, must have sounded like the tired voice of the repudiated Federalist conservatives. But those who dismissed him so casually failed to recognize that he was one of those who had brought a great revolution to success, who had shaped a Constitution built on revolutionary principles, and who had remained at heart a man convinced that inequality, the European caste system, and all the trappings of the *ancien régime* had no place in a New World, to whose peace and security he himself had contributed so much.

CHAPTER II

JAY, THE SUPREME COURT

AND THE SUBORDINATION

OF THE STATES

Was the Constitution destined to establish a national government that would be supreme over the states, or could the states in some areas preserve a complete and separate sovereignty unchecked and uncontrolled? The answer to that question rested, in the first place, on the provisions of the Constitution regarding the federal judiciary, and, in the second, on the early leadership of the Supreme Court bench.

As to the first, the Constitution in its final form provided, despite much concern voiced in the Convention over the judicial power which would be conferred upon the national government, that "the judicial power of the United States shall be vested in one Supreme Court, and in such inferior courts as the Congress may from time to time establish." Under the Articles the judicial power had been confined to appeals in prize cases, piracies and felonies on the high seas, and interstate disputes. Now the Constitution boldly extended that power to include "all cases, in law and equity, arising under this Constitution, the laws of the United States, and the treaties made, or which shall be made, under their authority; to all cases affecting ambassadors, other public ministers and consuls; to all cases of admiralty and maritime jurisdiction; to controversies to which the United States shall be a party; to controversies between two or more States; between a State and Citizens of another State; between Citizens of different States; between Citizens of the same State claiming lands under grants of different States, and between a State, or the Citizens thereof, and foreign States, Citizens or Subjects." [1]

On the second point, the character of the leadership of the Court, President Washington quickly reassured the country. Although Chancellor Livingston of New York and James Wilson of Philadelphia made no secret of their candidacy for the chief justiceship, and although the friends of John Rutledge of South Carolina put his name forward with much vigor, Washington preferred a close friend who was then secretary for foreign affairs. According to William Jay, John Jay's son, President Washington offered his father the choice of retaining his position as head of a major department or assuming the chief justiceship. [2] "It is with singular pleasure that I address you as Chief Justice of the Supreme Court of the United States, for which your commission is enclosed," wrote Washington to Jay. Recognizing the sacrifice that Jay was being asked to make, he added: "I have a full confidence that the love which you bear to our country, and a desire to promote the general happiness, will not suffer you to hesitate a moment to bring into action the talents, knowledge, and integrity which are so necessary to be considered as the keystone of our political fabric." [3]

At the time of the proffer of the chief justiceship Jay was only forty-four, and his legal and judicial experience had been relatively limited and remote from his current interests. His practice as a lawyer had ended in 1774 after a half dozen years, and his term as chief justice of New York had been even briefer. His was indeed a hard decision to make.

Although by temperament legalistic and cautious and possessed of sound judgment, Jay had in fact lost close contact
with the law. True, he had carried on after the war as an
executor of a number of important estates and later was to
counsel his son, Peter Augustus, when that young man was
admitted to practice, but he had handled great affairs of
state for many years, not litigation involving minor causes;
his interests if not his inclinations were more strongly bent
toward foreign affairs than toward adjudication. Furthermore, he had traveled widely and worked long and hard in
the service of the nation, and the labors on the high court
would involve the tedious circuit riding described in Jay's
manuscript Supreme Court diary, a routine that he loathed
and that he would find taxing to his health.[4] Despite these
limitations, his appointment was generally acceptable to the
nation as were the other nominees for the high bench.

The Supreme Court was not inundated at the start by
pressing litigation. The first and second terms of the Court
sitting in New York had no cases on the docket for argument. Still, it was at this strategic time that Jay made perhaps his most important contribution to the shaping of the
Court and to delimiting its scope. In November 1790, Alexander Hamilton, Secretary of the Treasury, submitted to him
the question of whether all the branches of the government
ought to intervene and assert their opposition to the principles of states' rights recently enunciated by the Virginia legislature. That body, under prodding from Patrick Henry,
had condemned Hamilton's proposal for the assumption of
the debts as unconstitutional. Hamilton sounded distraught
in his prompt reaction: "This is the first symptom of a spirit
which must either be killed, or will kill the Constitution of
the United States," he warned the Chief Justice. Hamilton's
feverish comment was no more out of character than was
Jay's cool response. Unlike Hamilton, Jay kept his head al-

though feeling was running high. Jay couched his reply to Hamilton in restrained language. He considered it inadvisable to take any action. "Having no apprehension of such measures, what was to be done appeared to me to be a question of some difficulty as well as importance; to treat them as very important might render them more so than I think they are . . . The assumption will do its own work; it will justify itself and not want advocates. Every indecent inference of State Assemblies will diminish their influence; the National Government has only to do what is right, and, if possible, be silent. If compelled to speak it should be in a few words, strongly evinced of temper, dignity, and self-respect." [5]

The fact that from the first the Jay court held strict views of the functions of the Court has served to distort the image of Jay and to contribute to the impression of students of the Court that the Chief Justice kept aloof from political issues. But one must carefully distinguish Jay the chief justice from Jay the Federalist statesman. In the former character Jay construed the functions of his Court as judicial rather than political or administrative. Thus, when in 1792 Congress passed an act providing that the circuit courts should pass on the claims of invalid pensioners, subject to review by the secretary of war and Congress, Jay and Cushing, sitting in the circuit court in New York, declared, in the first case to arise under the act, that "neither the Legislative nor the Executive branch can constitutionally assign to the Judicial any duties but such as are properly judicial, and to be performed in a judicial manner." In a compromise move to avoid a head-on collision with Congress over the issue of the Court's right to invalidate Congressional acts as well as to obviate hardship to bona fide claimants, they construed the act as in effect appointing the judges as commissioners to perform nonjudicial duties, thus accepting the duties but maintaining the principle. Having long labored to maintain the separation of powers, Jay must have been especially gratified when his views were upheld by Judges Wilson, Blair and Peters, sitting in the circuit court in Pennsylvania. The latter court in effect declared an act of Congress unconstitutional because it imposed nonjudicial duties on the judges and made their decisions subject to review by members of the executive branch of the government.[6]

The question of the Supreme Court taking a political position or rendering advisory opinions which might be construed as interfering with the legislative powers of Congress was raised once more and settled by Jay for all time. The expansion of the French Revolution into a general European war divided American opinion sharply. Steering an independent course, Washington in April of 1793 issued his notable Neutrality Proclamation, of which Jay had written an original draft. Meanwhile, numerous questions involving neutrality arose in American ports. At Washington's suggestion Secretary of State Thomas Jefferson wrote Jay on July 18, explaining that executive regulations regarding shipping and other aspects of neutrality involved delicate questions of interpretation of treaties. "The President," he said, "would be much relieved if he found himself free to refer questions of this description to the opinions of the judges of the Supreme Court." Their knowledge, Jefferson argued, "would secure us against errors dangerous to the peace of the United States, and their authority insure the respect of all parties." The Secretary of State passed along Washington's query on whether the judges might give advice on such questions, allowing them to strike out from the abstract questions proposed to them such as circumstances might, in their opinion, "forbid them to pronounce on."

Here was a trap quite unintentionally set for the Court,

and Jay evaded it with deliberation and dignity. He replied, first, that he would have to await those judges who were absent; then, on the assembling of the full court, he answered at great length on August 8. He pointed out that "the lines of separation drawn by the Constitution" provided checks upon each branch of the government by the other. Hence, since they were judges of a court of last resort they felt it improper to decide extrajudicially on such matters, "especially as the power given by the Constitution to the President, of calling on the heads of departments for opinions, seems to have been *purposely* as well as expressly united to the *executive* departments." His memorable argument was unanswerable, and that ended the matter.[7]

Jay's refusal to render advisory opinions represents only one side of the coin. By temperament an activist, Jay may have deemed it improper to have the Court perform extrajudicial functions or to get involved in political decision-making; but he himself did not hesitate while chief justice to give private advice to President Washington, heads of departments, and even the Senate. In 1792, when the first rumblings of discontent against the whisky tax had come out of western Pennsylvania, Jay urged Hamilton privately: "Let all the branches of government move together, and let the chiefs be committed publicly on one or the other side of the question." While the Chief Justice would not permit the Court to give formal advice on the executive regulations concerning neutrality, he himself counselled Washington to steer a neutral course, even preparing the original draft of the Proclamation of Neutrality. He also gave private legal advice regarding the stage at which a minister from revolutionary France might be received. In addition, he advised Senate committees on the interpretation of the Franco-American Treaty of Amity and Commerce and on the ransom of captives in Algiers, both topics with which Jay had been concerned as secretary for foreign affairs.[8]

In two other areas the Jay court laid down notable precedents. In the first, the Court established, temporarily at least, the subordination of the states to the national government in the matter of lawsuits. In the second, it asserted the supremacy of national treaties over state laws. Both of these decisions took courage, a quality which Jay possessed in full measure. He had been attacked in Congress years before for his independent role in negotiating the Treaty of Paris of 1782–1783. He had been stoned in the Doctors' Riot. He was later to be burned in effigy for his role as a principle in the negotiation of the treaty which bears his name. Jay had the intestinal fortitude to espouse a temporarily unpopular cause when, in his judgment, to do so was in keeping with the best interests of the nation.

Jay as chief justice had to make decisions on two moot issues. He had to rule on the suability of states in federal tribunals, and to uphold the supremacy of treaties. The first issue arose early in the history of the new nation and involved a variety of creditors with claims against the states. In one action a citizen of a foreign country brought suit against a state. The action was instituted against Maryland by Nicholas Van Staphorst, a partner of a Dutch financial house which had rendered aid to the state of Maryland and the continental government during and after the Revolution. The litigation stirred up a little pamphlet war. James Sullivan, who at that time was the attorney general of Massachusetts, and whose scholarly eminence rests on a study of land titles in that commonwealth, fired a broadside against the Supreme Court's entertaining this action even though Maryland had consented to the suit. "Sovereignty," he insisted, "must, in its nature, be absolute and uncontrollable by any civil authority, with respect to the objects to which it extends." The idea of a subordinate sovereignty Sullivan dismissed as nonsense. The United States might as well attempt to coerce the province of Nova Scotia as any of the states in the Union, he concluded. Sullivan drew an answer from a South Carolinian believed to be Timothy Ford, and it is ironical that a citizen of that state which was to stand for nullification in 1832 and for interposition by 1850 should, in 1791, have advocated the national supremacy. Ford argued that, while sovereignty is necessarily indivisible, the objects of sovereignty can be divided. The irony was compounded by Ford's shafts being directed against a states' rights upholder from Massachusetts. What a topsy-turvy situation history was to make of this!

Sullivan laid stress on the failure of Congress to authorize processes for suing a state. Ford, in reply, put the rhetorical question: "Is the non-existence of a power inferrable from a temporary non-user?" If a state were sued in a federal court and a judgment by default rendered against her, Ford argued, the force of public opinion within the state would rally against the legislature and the executive for overriding constitutional authority.[9] Clearly, Ford did not anticipate the behavior of some twentieth-century governors of the Deep South.

By January of 1792 Associate Justice James Iredell found it advisable to write to John Jay assigning reasons why the Chief Justice should not ride the southern circuit. He pointed out that the courts of North Carolina (his home state) had recently refused to obey a federal writ of certiorari issued at the instance of plaintiffs in an injunction suit pending before the state courts; further, the North Carolina assembly had gone on record expressing its thanks to the state judges for disobeying the federal writ. The honor of the United States was deeply concerned in the defiant

48

behavior of the state courts, Iredell remarked, and Jay's presence might cause him embarrassment, and humiliate the federal judiciary.[10]

It was in this superheated atmosphere of state defiance of the federal courts that the controversial decision of *Chisholm* v. *Georgia* came up to the Supreme Court; the decision evoked from the public as violent a reaction as any that was ever handed down by that high tribunal. *Chisholm* v. *Georgia* had the invidious distinction of being repudiated by constitutional amendment with much more expedition than two equally detested decisions—the Dred Scott and income tax cases.

Early reporters got the facts of *Chisholm* v. *Georgia* wrong, and later writers have perpetuated these errors. It did not involve a claim by either a Loyalist or a British creditor, as implied by Supreme Court reporter Alexander James Dallas. Dallas cited a Philadelphia dispatch from the *Salem* (Mass.) *Gazette* (perhaps the most remote secondhand authority ever accepted as a source in a sober judicial report). The suit was brought by the executors of a man named Farquhar, a citizen of South Carolina and a patriot, who, under contract with the governor and council of the state of Georgia in 1777 had supplied the state with cloth and clothing. The action was in assumpsit—a contractual remedy widely used for debt—and the damages sought amounted to the not inconsiderable sum of $69,613.33, South Carolina currency.[11]

The case first arose in the Georgia circuit court. On February 24, 1791, a summons was issued to the marshal of the district of Georgia, signed by the clerk of the federal circuit, requiring the state of Georgia to appear on April 25, 1791, to answer the plaintiff. On March 21 Governor Edward Telfair was served, and in October he entered a plea denying the jurisdiction of the court on the ground that Georgia was

49

a free and sovereign state. The plaintiff demurred, contending that the plea was insufficient in law and citing the Constitution to support his action. No one seems to have raised the point that the contract had been entered into ten years before the Constitution was adopted; but the reports of the first hearings are so fragmentary that we can barely piece together what actually transpired.[12]

After preliminary hearings in Georgia, the case was put on the Supreme Court calendar for the August 1792, term. On August 11 Attorney General Edmund Randolph, as counsel for the plaintiff, moved that judgment be entered against the state unless it should make its appearance at the next term. The Court, being anxious "to avoid every appearance of precipitancy and to give the State time to deliberate on the measures she ought to adopt," postponed consideration to the next term. The case came up for argument on February 5, 1793, the state of Georgia again refusing to appear and presenting a "written remonstrance and protestation" through Alexander J. Dallas and Jared Ingersoll of Pennsylvania, in which it denied the jurisdiction of the Court to entertain such a suit. Attorney General Randolph in a lengthy argument refuted the reasoning of the protest.

Randolph's refutation of the argument advanced in the "remonstrance" is important for two reasons. In the first place, it anticipated the reasoning of the majority of the Court; secondly, it revealed what Jefferson called his "chameleon" quality. Not an avowed Federalist, Randolph herein took an extreme high Federalist position. But perhaps this is a tribute to what has been called Randolph's "deep-seated capacity for vacillation."[13] He had refused to sign the Constitution while a member of the federal convention, but later supported it in the Virginia ratifying convention. His conduct as attorney general only succeeded in arousing the suspicions of Hamilton and Jefferson, now mortal antagonists.

Randolph held that the constitutional provision giving the Supreme Court jurisdiction in cases in which a state shall be a party, covered cases wherein the state was the defendant as well as the plaintiff. Listing many actions on the part of states expressly forbidden in the Constitution, he asked rhetorically: "Are states then to enjoy the high privilege of acting thus eminently wrong, without control; or does a remedy exist?" Protection against such unrestricted license, said the Attorney General, was rooted in morality, in the common-law principle that redress and punishment for infraction were inherent in any prohibition. Government, Randolph insisted, would be useless "if a pleasure to obey or transgress with impunity, should be substituted in the place of a sanction to its laws." The Founding Fathers had not intended citizens to be the victims of oppression by states, and thus the Constitution must have contemplated the right of an individual to sue a state.

Moving to different ground, Randolph supported the suability of states on "the relation in which the States stand to the Federal government." True, they were sovereignties, Randolph conceded, but the Constitution "derives its origin immediately from the people; and the people individually are, under certain limitations, subject to the legislative, executive, and judicial authorities thereby established." The states are in fact assemblages of these individuals who are liable to process. "Such limitations as the Federal Government is permitted to impose upon their powers" Randolph declared to be "diminutions of sovereignty, at least equal to the making of them defendants." The Articles of Confederation, Randolph admitted, had not granted federal jurisdiction over the states; yet he denied any weight to this analogy, declaring that "that scanty and strict paper was of so different a hue and feature from the Constitution as scarcely to appear the child of the same family." Holding it "no degradation of sovereignty in the States to submit to the Supreme Judiciary of the United States," Randolph argued that, "it did not follow, however, that the United States might be sued. The head of the confederacy," he contended, "is not within the reach of the judicial authorities of its inferior members. It is exempted by its peculiar preeminence."

The Judiciary Act of 1789 conferred on the Supreme Court jurisdiction over controversies "where a State shall be a party." This jurisdiction, Randolph maintained, was extended without making any distinction between a state as plaintiff and as defendant. A corollary to such jurisdiction, however, must be the court's power to execute judgment against a state. This power, it was objected, had not been granted by the Constitution, the Judiciary Act, or by special legislation. Randolph countered this objection by reference to the fourteenth section of the Judiciary Act, which empowered the Court to issue all writs necessary for the exercise of its jurisdiction. This power, he held, should apply to individual suits against states as well as to suits between states, about which no question of the court's jurisdiction had ever been raised. Even were such an interpretation of the Judiciary Act not acceptable, said Randolph, the authority to execute judgment arose from the Court's incidental powers.

Would states resist such an execution? Randolph averted his glance from the "painful possibilities" arising from such a contingency. "Rather, let us hope and pray," he said, "that not a single star in the *American* constellation will ever suffer its lustre to be dimmed by hostility against the sentence of a court which itself has adopted." [14]

The Court rendered its decision before a large audience on February 18, 1793. The majority upheld its jurisdiction over the case, Iredell alone dissenting. Georgia was to appear and show cause to the contrary at the next term of court or judgment would be entered by default against the state. Georgia complied by sending Dallas and Ingersoll to the next term with a request for postponement of the argument on judgment. This was granted. The argument was heard in February of 1794; notwithstanding, the Court, with Iredell absent, unanimously decided that judgment be entered. On Randolph's motion a writ of inquiry was awarded to ascertain the plaintiff's damages.[15] Six months later the Court directed a jury to be summoned to determine the damages sustained by the plaintiff by reason of the nonperformance of the assumption.[16] In February of 1795, the notation was made. Randolph's clients, however, agreed that "this cause should continue open." This delay may have been prompted by the action then pending on the ratification of the Eleventh Amendment.

Both John Blair and William Cushing, two of the four members composing the majority, brought years of legal and adjudicatory experience to the Supreme Court bench. Since independence, each had served on the highest court of his state—Blair in Virginia, Cushing in Massachusetts. Both had strongly supported ratification of the Constitution. During the confederation years, Cushing had won an unenviable reputation for enforcing the claims of creditors despite bitter criticism.[17] His service on the Massachusetts bench was marked by continued reaffirmation of the authority of government and of the state constitution; his decisions upheld contractual engagements and the public credit, especially where pledged in the revolutionary cause.[18] During Shays' Rebellion he sternly denounced the demands for paper money as "repugnant to all honesty—to the righteousness which exalteth a Nation." [19]

One would expect these two learned gentlemen to take a strict legalistic view and to vote to uphold contracts and the supremacy of the nation over the states on this issue. That expectation was not ill-founded. Blair concluded that a proper reading of the Constitution supported the Court's jurisdiction. "No state in the Union," he insisted, "should, by withholding justice, have it in its power to embroil the whole confederacy in disputes of another nature." Along with Blair, Cushing held that the phrase, "controversies between a State and Citizens of another State," applied equally whether a demand was made against or by a state. Cushing was not disturbed by the argument that conferring such a jurisdiction on the Supreme Court would "reduce States to mere corporations." All states were corporations, he pointed out, and their sovereignty was necessarily abridged where power was vested in the federal government for the general good.[20]

Of all those gracing the federal bench at this time James Wilson, the dour Scotsman from Pennsylvania, was the most knowledgeable about what we would today call political science. One of the most learned expositors of the rights of the colonies against Parliament, Wilson had early played up the sovereignty of the people and played down that of the states. His Revolutionary War pamphlets made a strong case for popular sovereignty and indicted the Parliament for overstepping the powers allegedly granted to it by the people of the colonies. "That all power was originally in the people," he had asserted, "that all powers of government are derived from them, that all power which they have not disposed of still continues theirs, are maxims of the English Constitution which, we presume, will not be disputed."[21]

Wilson's removal from frontier Pennsylvania to Philadelphia brought a change in his clientele from Scotch-Irish farmers of the west to larger business entrepreneurs, big companies, and Loyalist claimants; a corresponding conservative coloration to his political outlook also became apparent. Long recognized as a stalwart adherent of popular sovereignty, the Associate Justice was equally stalwart in his support of national authority. His pamphlets written during the confederation period reflect his consistent belief that sovereignty was vested in the general government of the Union and not in the states.[22] In the federal convention he had urged that "the national legislative powers ought to flow immediately from the people, so as to contain all their understanding, and to be an exact transcript of their minds." He heartily endorsed the popular election of the House of Representatives, preferring this method for the Senate as well. Wilson opposed the doctrine of equal representation of states in the Upper House: "Can we forget for whom we are forming a Government? Is it for men, or for the imaginary beings called *States?* Will our honest constituents be satisfied with metaphysical distinctions?" [23] In the debates he continued to assert that the "General Government" was not "an assemblage of states, but of individuals for certain political purposes," that it was not meant for the states, but for the individuals composing them, and that the individuals and not the states ought to be represented in it. His identification with popular sovereignty made it seem logical for him to advocate representation in proportion to population in both houses of Congress.[24]

Was the state, in Wilson's thinking, to have any future role? Wilson looked upon the states as analogous to the shires and counties of England, considering them as administrative subdivisions rather than sovereign entities.[25]

Wilson had made no secret of his national views. From the debates in the Pennsylvania convention one might easily have predicted just how Wilson would cast his vote in the case of *Chisholm* v. *Georgia*. In the debates over ratification Wilson made direct reference to the provision of the judiciary article of the Constitution which conferred jurisdiction upon the judicial branch over controversies "between a state and citizens of another state" (Art. III, sect. 2). "When this power is attended to," he observed, "it will be found to be a necessary one. Impartiality is the leading feature in this Constitution; it pervades the whole. When a citizen has a controversy with another state, there ought to be a tribunal where both parties may stand on a just and equal footing." He set forth a similar point of view in the law lectures he delivered at the College of Philadelphia. "Is a man degraded by the manly declaration that he renders himself amenable to justice?" he asked his students. "Can a similar declaration degrade a state?" [26]

In view of his nationalist background, Wilson's opinion in *Chisholm v. Georgia* contained few surprises. At the outset he enunciated his doctrine that sovereignty resided in the people, that the state was made for man, not man for the state, and that there was nothing in its nature or definition which should exclude it from liability to suit. *"As to the purposes of Union,"* he contended, *"Georgia is not a sovereign state,"* and could make no claim of sovereign exemption or immunity. Insisting that the Constitution was established by the people, he argued that the people in the states could diminish, extinguish, or transfer former state powers.[27]

The Chief Justice was well known to share James Wilson's views of nationalist power; he had gone on record as considering the states mere subdivisions, not separate sovereignties. From John Jay one might therefore expect a broad restatement of the national authority and of the sovereignty of the people in tune with Wilson's. Further, he could be expected to place his arguments in a broad philosophical context rather than to confine himself to narrow legalistic reasoning. Jay's strong nationalism had until now found its best exposition in his notable *Address to the People of the State of New York,* urging ratification of the Constitution. His memorable and impolitic opinion in *Chisholm v. Georgia* strongly buttressed his earlier views.

Jay was disposed neither to cramp the federal judicial power nor to augment the claims for the sovereignty of the respective states. Toward the latter he adopted a line very similar to Wilson's, contending that the sovereignty of the country as a whole passed from the Crown of Great Britain to the people of the colonies once the Declaration of Independence was adopted. At first "in the hurry of the war, and in the warmth of mutual confidence," they based their general government upon "a confederation of the States." But the confederation was soon found lacking, and "the people, in their collective and national capacity, established the present Constitution." Pointing to the opening phrase in the preamble of the Constitution, "We, the people of the United States, do ordain and establish this Constitution," Jay regarded this as evidence that the people had acted as "sovereigns of the whole country." On this point Jay concluded that "the sovereignty of the nation is in the people of the nation, and the residuary sovereignty of each State in the people of each State." Biographers of Jay have, with good reason, made the point that the Chief Justice's determination of the locus of sovereignty anticipated by twenty-six years Marshall's classic finding in *McCulloch* v. *Maryland* that "the Government of the Union, then is emphatically and truly a government of the people." [28]

To Jay none of the reasons which rendered European sovereigns immune to suits in their own courts applied to America, where the citizens themselves were "joint-tenants" in sovereignty and governments derived their authority from the people. Hence, in Jay's mind, there was no incompatibility between suability and state sovereignty. If a municipality like Philadelphia could be sued, why not a state? Why it should be "more incompatible that all the people of a state should be sued by one citizen than by one hundred thousand," Jay failed to perceive. If, collectively, the people of one state could sue the people, collectively, of another, then why should not an individual have the right to sue the people in their collective capacity? Indeed, "that rule is said to be a bad one," Jay remarked, "which does not work both ways."

Considering the design of the Constitution, Jay pointed out that the danger of interstate animosities and even hostilities such as had occurred under the Confederation made a common tribunal desirable, "from motives both of justice and policy." By taking our place as a nation we became amenable to the law of nations; it had been proven inexpedient to refer international issues to state courts, particularly to the courts of delinquent states. The federal government thus offered a tribunal in which the states could demand that justice be done *to* them; surely, Jay argued, it should provide a means to exact justice *by* them as well. This should not be by violence and force, "but in a stable, sedate, and regular course of judicial procedure."

Then reexamining the purposes of the Constitution as stated in the preamble, he asked, "What is the precise sense and latitude in which the words 'to establish justice,' as here used, are to be understood?" Ten types of cases, Jay explained, had been set aside by the Constitution as most effectively dealt with by the federal judiciary; in each case a national tribunal could best satisfy the ends, set forth by the people in the constitutional preamble, of foreign and domestic tranquillity, of justice, of popular sovereignty, of the equal rights of men. It was desirable, he insisted, for the federal government to have jurisdiction over "controversies between a state, or the citizens thereof," and "foreign nations or people." Similarly the national authority should be invoked in "controversies between a State and Citizens of another State." This was certainly proper when the state was plaintiff, for in this way the "suspicions of partiality" of a state's court toward its own citizens could be avoided.

Jay felt that this clause should be construed liberally and not be restricted to cases in which the state was the plaintiff. If it had been really intended to confine the judicial power only to controversies wherein a state was plaintiff, the terms of the grant would surely have been so defined and limited. Instead, Jay found "not even an intimation of such intention" in any part of the Constitution.

Jay now reached treacherous ground. His argument supporting the suability of states by private citizens in federal courts had been based on the notion of the sovereignty of the people and its compatibility with suability, the settled principle of equal justice for all, and a fair and reasonable construction of the words "controversies" and "party." If, as he was forced now to concede, the Constitution also extended the federal judicial power to "controversies to which the United States shall be a party," would it not logically follow that the totality of his argument might be applicable against the United States as well? Ideally, Jay admitted, it would be desirable if "the whole nation could, in the peaceable course of law, be compelled to do justice, and be sued by individual citizens." But there is an important difference, he noted, between actions against states or individual citizens, and actions against the United States. In all cases in the former category the national courts are supported by the executive power of the United States; but in causes of action against the United States, "there is no power which the courts can call to their aid."

In conclusion, Jay urged that the extension of the judiciary power of the United States to controversies like those in *Chisholm* v. *Georgia* appeared to him "to be *wise,* because it is *honest,* and because it is *useful.*" Not only does it secure "individual citizens as well as States, in their respective rights, but it leaves not even the most obscure and friendless citizen without means of obtaining justice from a neighboring State." Furthermore, "it recognizes and rests upon this great moral truth, that justice is the same whether due from one man to a million, or from a million to one man." Finally, it brings to the fore the great principle of the sovereignty of the people.[29]

The majority had spoken, forcefully, eloquently, and audaciously. It remained for the dissenter to have the last word. James Iredell's entire professional and public career as lawyer, judge, attorney general, and Federalist leader prior to his elevation to the Supreme Court, had been confined to the domain of North Carolina. A moderate with national inclinations, he could not be oblivious to the extreme states' rights point of view prevailing in his state. He could not ignore the fact that his state had been one of the very last to ratify and that it had withheld its approval until after the Bill of Rights had been proposed to the states by the new Congress. Also, North Carolina, in flagrant violation of the treaty of peace, had continued to confiscate and sell Tory property, to proscribe former British sympathizers, to reject all Tory claims for restitution, and to impede the satisfaction of British creditors. In addition, it had emitted a mass of paper money and securities, and by 1790 its per capita public debt was second among the states. Nowhere was the Judiciary Act of 1789 more vehemently denounced, and nowhere else was there a greater demand for reform of the judicial system which had only just been inaugurated.[30] So intense was the hostility to federal jurisdiction in North Carolina that in 1790 the members of the lower house of its legislature refused to take an oath to support the Constitution.[31] The intensity of states' rights feeling could not have been lost on Iredell and indubitably was reflected in his carefully reasoned dissenting opinion.

Aside from the power of its reasoning, what lends special distinction to Iredell's dissent is that it soon became the law of the land by a ringing popular affirmation. Iredell's public stand on the jurisdiction of the federal judiciary suggested the direction his opinion would take. Replying to George Mason's antifederalist pamphlet, *Objections . . . to the Proposed Federal Constitution,* the North Carolinian asserted that "in no case, but where the Union is in some measure concerned, are the federal courts to have any jurisdiction." [32]

Iredell took a narrow legalistic view, arguing the proposition that no action in assumpsit or for the recovery of money could be brought in the federal courts against a state. He argued that despite the judicial authority given the Court by the Constitution, such authority could not be exercised in the absence of explicit congressional legislation. "The whole business of organizing the courts, and directing the methods of their proceedings, where necessary," Iredell conceived "to be in the discretion of Congress." Iredell may well have been influenced by the opinion expressed by Hamilton in the 28th *Federalist.* Therein he asserted that the legislature "prescribed the rules by which the duties and rights of every citizen are to be regulated," and denied to the judiciary any "active resolution." Of the federal judiciary, Hamilton declared, "it may be truly said to have neither FORCE nor WILL, but merely judgment." [33]

Having made the point that it was necessary for Congress to effectuate the constitutional grant of judicial authority before the Court could act in any matter, Iredell then argued that such power in the case at hand had not in fact been granted. He contended that any writs issued by the Court "must be agreeable to the principles and usages of law," that no state had on the books a law authorizing a compulsory suit for recovery against itself, and that no precedent could be found in the common law. Departing from this narrow construction of the Constitution and the Judiciary Act, which implied that Congress possessed the power to confer such jurisdiction but had not actually done so, Iredell insisted that, except where its sovereignty had been delegated to the United States, the state was "completely sovereign." "The United States are sovereign as to all the powers of government actually surrendered: each state in the Union is sovereign, as to all the powers reserved."

Iredell furthermore insisted that the Judiciary Act conferred on the Supreme Court only concurrent not exclusive jurisdiction in such cases, and that the Supreme Court was intended to exercise only such jurisdiction as a state court could have exercised in like cases at the time that the Judiciary Act was passed. The question now to be examined was: Could such a suit at common law have been entertained in Georgia against that state prior to 1789? After an exhaustive examination of the English authorities, he concluded that a petition of right was the only avenue by which a subject could pursue a claim against the Crown. Iredell went on to deny the legitimacy of any analogy between subordinate corporations in their relation to the British government and the American states in their relation to the federal government; for a corporation's charter could be forfeited by abuse or revoked by an act of the legislature, whereas a state, "though subject in certain specified particulars to the authority of the government of the United States, is, in every other respect, totally independent from it." [34]

In passing, it might be pointed out that, so far as the Supreme Court's original jurisdiction is concerned, later courts have held it to have been conferred by the Constitution; but as regards other jurisdiction, Iredell's rule has been observed.[35] To give effect to the judicial power, legislative authorization and direction are considered necessary.[36]

Memoranda left by Iredell, though forming no part of his opinion, underscore his constitutional thinking on this issue.[37] The failure of the Constitutional Convention explicitly to bar suits by an individual against a state was interpreted by Jay, Cushing, and Randolph as supporting their argument; Iredell, however, inferred from the silence of the Constitution a contrary conclusion. Are we justified, he asked, in forcing such a construction on the framers of the Constitution? "If ever there was a case in which the Convention should have spoken out explicitly" Iredell contended, "this certainly was the case—where whole Sovereignties are to be brought to a bar of justice in the very same manner and without any distinction as single individuals. But it will be remembered, that the authority, not existing before, did not continue, unless excluded: it does not exist if not conveyed by this instrument."

Iredell's rebuttal of the reasoning of the majority was a shrewd and skillful poltical operation. He did not foreswear his Federalist viewpoint. He did not impugn the sovereignty of the people, or the sovereignty of the Union as to those powers delegated to it under the Constitution, or the power of the people of the United States to limit the sovereignty of the states in any respect they might choose. He merely reminded the majority that, though possessed of that power, the people had not intended to confer such jurisdiction and had not done so in fact or law.

Many other Federalist leaders were aware of the danger the principle of state sovereignty posed to the new federal government. Hamilton in the 32nd *Federalist* paper had spoken of "the extreme hazard of provoking the resentments of the State governments," and Madison in subsequent

Federalist numbers had made a point of the reserved powers of the states under the federal system. He had been joined by John Marshall in giving assurances to the Virginia convention that a state could not be sued by private citizens. In the course of the debates in Virginia over the ratification of the Constitution, Marshall had expressed the hope "that no gentleman will think that a state will be called at the bar of a Federal court." "It is not rational," he asserted, "to suppose that the Sovereign power should be dragged before a court. The intent is to enable states to recover claims of individuals residing in other states." If there were partiality in this, "if an individual" could not "obtain judgment against a state, though he may be sued by a state," then it was a difficulty which to Marshall could "not be avoided." The claimant's only recourse, as Marshall saw it, was by application for relief to the state legislature.[38]

Now the direct collision that Marshall had dreaded had in fact occurred, and all because Jay and Wilson allowed their strong nationalist feeling to get the better of their political caution.

Chisholm v. *Georgia* burst like a bomb upon an unsuspecting nation and evoked an immediate response from states' rights supporters in all parts of the country.[39] Georgia's lower house passed a bill fixing a penalty of hanging for any person assisting in the enforcement of the Court's decree, and followed this up with a declaration setting forth that portion of her sovereignty which the state of Georgia claimed to have retained.[40] From Massachusetts, which had recently been named defendant in a similar action (*Vassal* v. *Massachusetts*), came an instruction of the General Court to its senators and representatives in Congress "to adopt the most speedy and effectual measures in their power to obtain such amendments in the Constitution of the United States as will remove any clause or article of the said Constitution which can be construed to imply or justify a decision that a State is compellable to answer in any suit by an individual or individuals in the courts of the United States." The legislatures of Connecticut and Virginia instructed their senators and representatives along identical lines.[41]

The move to amend the Constitution was pressed with celerity. On February 20, 1793, just two days after the Court rendered its decision, a motion was introduced in the Senate proposing the following amendment to the Constitution: "The judicial power of the United States shall not extend to any suit in law or equity, commenced or prosecuted against one of the United States by citizens of another State, or by citizens or subjects of any foreign State." [42] The next Congress at its very first session, on January 2, 1794, made a significant change in the wording of the proposed amendment. Instead of "the judicial power of the United States shall not extend" the phrase was changed to read "shall not be construed to extend." In this form it received the approval of the Senate on January 14, 1794, by a vote of 23 to 2, and of the House on March 4, 1794, by a vote of 81 to 9.[43] All attempts to revise the amendment were voted down, and by early 1798, within four years after its initiation, the Eleventh Amendment had received the necessary ratification by the states. On January 8 of that year, the President formally proclaimed it law in his message to Congress.[44]

The Eleventh Amendment raised some broader questions which remained to vex the Court. Was it meant to prevent suits by individuals against states raising the legality or constitutionality of state action? Did the amendment prohibit suits brought against a state by its own citizens? Time and the Court itself would give the answers to these important questions. It is sufficient at this time to consider briefly a few of the broader historical and constitutional implications of *Chisholm v. Georgia.* Though couched in conservative Federalist language, the Iredell opinion may be said to have laid the legal and judicial foundation for the states' rights doctrines which, carried to their extreme, worked an exercise in tragic futility. In time and logic they anticipated the Virginia and Kentucky Resolves of Madison and Jefferson, the views of certain extreme Federalists during the War of 1812, South Carolina's nullification ordinance, the legal foundations of the principles of secession, and, more recently, the fallacious doctrine of interposition advanced to support bigotry and the continued denial of equality to Americans of one race. Perhaps this is unfair to the judicious James Iredell, who was soberly voicing what was in large measure a consensus of the framers of the Constitution: that it was intended to create a federal union in which sovereignty would be divided between the federal government and the states. Iredell had epitomized this view of federalism in his charge to the grand jury of the circuit court for the district of Georgia in April 1792:

We ought never to forget that there are two governments to which we owe obedience; each limited but each perfect in its kind: the State governments, in all instances of authority not relinquished to the United States; and the Government of the United States in all instances of authority so relinquished and of which the Constitution of the United States forms the evidence and the barrier.[45]

The source of that division of authority which Iredell and most of the Founding Fathers recognized remained undefined and indefinite. Were the states as separate political entities to delegate the authority, as Iredell urged, or was the source to be derived from the people of the United States as one national entity, as Jay and Wilson had argued? James Wilson was right when he called this "a case of uncommon magnitude," for the question was not settled then, and it still presents problems of enormous magnitude. Federalists like Hamilton, Jay, and Wilson, in their anxiety to quiet the fears of the opponents of the Constitution, had each on occasion played up the divided sovereignty of the nation. Yet a vibrant note of national supremacy runs through their writings at this time, possibly in least diluted form in the remarks attributed to John Jay.

The minority opinion in *Chisholm* v. *Georgia,* given Constitutional sanction in the Eleventh Amendment, dominated the constitutional thinking of the early decades of the nineteenth century, the heroic labors of Chief Justice Marshall to affirm and advance the national interpretation notwithstanding. Lest we be carried away by the logic of states' rights, we must bear in mind the cautions of so authoritative an expounder of the Constitution as James Madison. In the 45th *Federalist* Madison declared: "It is too early for politicians to presume on our forgetting that the public good, the real welfare of the great body of the people, is the supreme object to be pursued; and that no form of government whatever has any other value than as it may be fitted for the attainment of this object." So "far as the sovereignty of the States cannot be reconciled to the happiness of the people," Madison concluded, "the voice of every good citizen must be, Let the former be sacrificed to the latter." True, Madison sang a different tune in 1798 from that he had sounded ten years earlier, but his original words have more pertinence to the welfare state and the nuclear and space age than some of his later notions.

John Jay and James Iredell had sought a modus vivendi whereby the nation could function part-federal, part-national. We are still wrestling with that delicate problem.

Adjudication arising under the Eleventh Amendment curtailed state sovereignty, which the amendment's sponsors had sought to perpetuate. On the question of whether the amendment barred Supreme Court review of judgments obtained *by* states *against* private parties whose defense under the Constitution or federal law had been overruled by a lower court, Chief Justice Marshall, in *Cohens* v. *Virginia* answered with an emphatic negative.[46]

Did the Eleventh Amendment settle the question of the right of private parties to sue a state? Not entirely. In later years attempts were made by subterfuge to secure access to the federal courts for suits against states. Since the Eleventh Amendment did not bar one state from suing another, six creditors of the state of Louisiana who were citizens of New Hampshire assigned their debts to the latter state, evidently to have it act as a collection agency for them. The Court held that New Hampshire was not a real party to the suit, and that the Court, therefore, did not have jurisdiction.[47] In another instance, however, the owner of certain bonds issued by North Carolina, which were in default, donated the bonds to South Dakota. When South Dakota brought suit in the Supreme Court to collect the bonds, the Court decided in its favor on the ground that the state in this case was the real party and therefore entitled to sue.[48]

It has been suggested by one eminent constitutional authority that the losses resulting from the inability of individuals to sue states have not been great, and that states, whether on the grounds of improved ethical standards or of business expediency, have usually fulfilled their clear obligations. He feels that "the elimination of friction" may well have justified enactment of the constitutional amendment.[49] However true this may be of recent years, the proposition is hardly supportable for the early national and ante-bellum periods. After the panic of 1837, overextension, corruption, maladministration, and other factors accentuated a crisis in which five states temporarily defaulted on their interest payments and one partially repudiated the principal of its debt. The result was a drying up of the foreign market for American securities and a virtual cessation of work on public improvements in some of the western states.

Since *Chisholm* v. *Georgia* and the Eleventh Amendment, the Supreme Court has moved far along the path of nationalism. In its construction of three key clauses of the Constitution—the necessary-and-proper clause, the general-welfare clause, and the commerce clause—the Court has expanded the powers of the national government in areas where the states once stood supreme. The Fourteenth Amendment and the recent broad construction of the Bill of Rights as safeguarding citizens from actions of the states as well as of the federal government have in fact revolutionized federal–national relations and upset the delicate balance that some of the framers, if not all of them, sought to maintain. It has brought the nation much closer to John Jay's ideas than it was during his own lifetime.

The passage of the Eleventh Amendment was a major factor in persuading Jay (wrongly as it turned out) that the Supreme Court would not have great influence in the national life, and in dissuading him from accepting reappointment as chief justice from President John Adams. Had he returned to the bench in 1801—and one must remember that he lived until 1829—most of the nationalist decisions that emanated from the pen of John Marshall would very probably have been written by Jay, whose views Marshall so completely shared. Jay's reputation as a constitutional statesman would have been vastly enhanced thereby.

For its decision in *Chisholm* v. *Georgia* the Jay court was traduced by a vast section of the country. So was the Taney court, and with better reason (for the Dred Scott decision); even more vehemently has the Warren court been assailed for *Brown* v. *Board of Education* and its notable line of civil liberties' decisions. Yet, were Jay alive today he would perhaps have the satisfaction of knowing that the Eleventh Amendment could never be rammed through Congress and the states in the fashion that it was in the 1790's. The states no longer loom so large in the scheme of things. The huge fiscal burdens that government is now called upon to shoulder and the complex and wide-ranging operations it is expected to assume have in effect transformed federal–state relations, redistributing power in a way that could only be highly gratifying to John Jay.[50]

What is notable and lasting about the majority opinion in *Chisholm* v. *Georgia,* so quickly overruled by constitutional amendment, is that it raised the crucial question of the base upon which the powers of the federal government rested. Did these powers emanate from the states or from the people as a whole? Jay and Wilson had declared the people to be the source of authority. In the years to come, when the states' rights doctrine threatened the cause of national unity, Jay's position in *Chisholm* v. *Georgia* was continually called to mind and reaffirmed. On the Supreme Court bench John Marshall asserted the people to be the source of authority in decisions such as *McCulloch* v. *Maryland;* Daniel Webster proclaimed it from the floor of the Senate; and Chief Justice Chase reaffirmed the doctrine in the years which followed the Civil War. The conclusion of that terrible conflict would finally vindicate Jay's concept, set forth seventy years before, of one nation and one people, consisting of "free and equal citizens," with "equal justice for all." [51]

CHAPTER III

JAY, THE SUPREME COURT,

AND THE SUPREMACY

OF TREATIES

Chisholm v. *Georgia* reflects fairly the thinking of the
Chief Justice on the issue of the sovereignty of the individual states. In his efforts to forge a doctrine of national
supremacy Jay seized upon another hotly contested issue,
the enforceability by the national government of private
debts honored by the Treaty of Paris of 1783, to which he
had been a party. These prewar debts had proved uncollect-
ible in state courts.

The problem of debts to Loyalists and to English and
Scottish businessmen was complex, and its moral aspects
overlaid with economic and political considerations. The
debt issue arose at the very start of the Revolution when
normal trade relations between the British Isles and America were severed. At the outbreak of the war colonial indebtedness to Great Britain exceeded five million pounds,
perhaps two pounds sterling per capita. Not a huge sum
admittedly, but the debt was maldistributed and hit one
region of the thirteen states hardest: the bulk of the debtors
were Southerners, with Virginians standing in the front
rank. The Virginia planters had incurred their obligations
to British traders and factors in the course of transactions

involving the sale of tobacco overseas. The debt of the Virginians alone amounted to over two million pounds or forty per cent of the total.[1]

This debt of the tobacco-raising states was not, it should be remembered, a sudden phenomenon, but could be traced back to the decade 1761–1770, when the tobacco provinces experienced an adverse balance of trade with England. That adverse balance amounted to £23 million for that decade alone. The economic distress of Virginia in the pre-Revolutionary period prompted its legislature to issue treasury notes which were deemed full legal tender. These new notes frightened English and Scottish merchants who feared that their sterling debts would depreciate thereby. They did not necessarily close the door to all paper, but wanted to retain the option to accept paper money or to refuse it. To check the paper-money heresy in America, Parliament passed the Currency Act in 1764. The measure, by forbidding payment of sterling debts in paper money, struck a blow at legal tender currency; the result pleased neither the Virginia debtors nor their overseas creditors.[2] By the beginning of the Revolution the Virginians, accustomed to what seemed to be an unenviable state of permanent indebtedness, were equally accustomed to seeking relief through laws passed in their legislature regulating the exchange rate between Virginia currency and sterling. By such legal devices they sought to write off a portion of their debts.[3]

Indebtedness was the lot of both the larger planters and the yeomen farmers. Both groups shared the perilous dependence on great expectations, hoping with each crop that the proceeds would bail them out of debt. Accompanying the dangerously mounting credit inflation was a scarcity of money which made it increasingly difficult for planters to pay their debts by the sale of slaves, land, or other assets. When news reached America that the treaty of peace provided that creditors on either side should meet with no lawful impediment to the recovery in full value of their debts, a furor broke out in Virginia. The patriot George Mason wrote Patrick Henry that the question was frequently raised in conversation: "If we are now to pay the debts due the British merchants, what have we been fighting for all this while?" [4]

There is, however, respectable evidence that all debtors did not think alike on this issue. Richard Randolph's reaction to the implication that he would not meet his obligations was not untypical of many Virginians. Randolph rebuked his creditors, the Bristol firm of Farrell and Jones, for holding his "Honour" in "so little Esteem." And Burges Ball wrote the merchant Duncan Campbell that "you may rely that no private advantage shall be thought of by me, and I hope that matters will e'er long be friendly determined."

Leading Virginians were divided over the justice of using the weapon of nonpayment of debts as a political instrument to force repeal of the "Coercive Acts." Washington thought nonpayment should be employed only in the last resort, and Robert Beverly judged such action "full of cruelty and injustice." Among those opposed to withholding debts were such other considerable figures as Paul Carrington, Carter Braxton, Edmund Pendleton, Thomas Nelson, Jr., and Peyton Randolph. On the other hand, Mason, Henry, Richard Henry Lee, and Robert Carter Nicholas supported nonpayment of debts, and one modern writer suggests that the latter group represented a majority of Virginians.[5]

Regardless of whether Virginians considered these obligations as debts of honor, they managed to make it difficult if not impossible for the creditors to collect them.

First, their Revolutionary state legislature adopted resolutions deporting all foreign merchants "except only such of them as have heretofore uniformly manifested a friendly disposition to the American cause, or are attached to this country by having wives or children here." [6] Secondly, a series of laws made the state government's paper money legal currency for the payment of debts. Thirdly, to aid the financing of the war and to appease debtors who claimed that hostile merchants still refused the paper money and were thus driving it down to a new lower level, the legislature enacted a general sequestration law in October 1777, providing that debts due British subjects from citizens of Virginia could be paid into the loan office of the state, and that the auditor would give the debtor a certificate of payment that would discharge the debtor of all future obligations to the creditor. [7] Since paper money was by this date worth one-third its face value and since it was depreciating ominously each day, the advantages to the debtor in making a payment into the loan office were enormous. Finally, paper money depreciated so drastically in value that the assembly in its May session in 1780 felt obliged to repeal the law providing for payments into the loan office. However, by this date large sums had been paid in and certificates of discharge in significant amounts turned over to the complying debtors. In fact, between January and May, 1780, when the payments were stopped, £139,307 had been paid to the state, most of it when one pound sterling was equivalent to sixty pounds of the Virginia currency. In all, the state treasury received £273,554 of paper money, with a sterling value of £15,044, to discharge British debts. In effect, this device amounted to a settlement on an eighteen-to-one basis, on average—virtual repudiation. [8]

John Jay's interest in the debt issue went back to the negotiations of 1782–1783 which culminated in the Treaty of Paris. *The Peacemakers* details how Franklin, Jay, and John Adams, the American peace commissioners, confronted the seasoned diplomats of Europe, countered their devious stratagems, and brilliantly negotiated that treaty which ended the Revolutionary War and procured independence for the United States. Richard Oswald, Britain's peace commissioner to the Americans, had been instructed from the beginning to secure redress for British creditors, along with the restitution or indemnification of Loyalists whose properties had been confiscated. However, with the death of the Marquess of Rockingham and the accession of Lord Shelburne to the post of prime minister, the British government came to feel that it might be able to drive a wedge between America and her French ally by offering surprisingly favorable terms. On August 29, 1782, the cabinet instructed Oswald to waive stipulating by treaty for payment of prewar debts owing to British merchants as well as compensation to the Tories if he felt it necessary to do so.

The British ministry counted on world opinion to bring about an equitable settlement of both issues. But following the failure of the Spaniards to raise the siege of Gibraltar in September and October, the British government stiffened its terms toward both the Americans and the French. The draft treaty that Jay drew up and that Oswald submitted to his government omitted mention of both the Tories and the debts. The British cabinet was then under insistent pressure from a variety of interests—Canadian fur traders, English fishermen, American Tories, and, not the least, English and Scottish creditors. To conciliate these very vocal groups a new set of instructions was given to Oswald in October. He was called upon to urge the Americans "as strongly as possible" to discharge their prewar debts. Henceforth, the debts, along with the fisheries and the claims of the Tories were the chief points at issue between the British and American negotiators. Shelburne insisted that *"honest* debts be *honestly* paid in *honest* money," ruling out "Congress money"; he was doubtless aware of the practice prevalent in Virginia where debts due British merchants were discharged by depreciated local currency paid to the state loan office. He ignored the fact that, while the debts owed to English merchants were usually payable in sterling, those to Glasgow businessmen often specified colonial currencies. Fearing unfavorable treatment of British debtors in the local courts, Shelburne wanted some assurance that appeals could be taken to a federal tribunal.

Had the negotiations remained entirely in the hands of Franklin and Jay it is possible that no concession on the debt question would have been made by the Americans. However, at the end of October John Adams joined his two colleagues, and at once, in what seems to have come as an offhand and even impulsive gesture, he indicated privately to the British that he would put no impediment in the way of the collection of debts. "I have no notion of cheating anybody," he asserted. He did this without advance consultation with either Jay or Franklin, both of whom had been insisting for months that both the commissioners and Congress lacked the power to deal with the subject. Now that Adams chose to put the debt issue on high moral ground, Franklin saw it was useless to protest. Adams persuaded his colleagues to accept a formula whereby Congress would recommend that the states open their courts of justice for the recovery of all just debts, and John Jay drafted the article as it appears in the treaty.

Article 4 reads: "It is agreed that creditors on either side shall meet with no lawful impediment to the recovery of the full value in sterling money of all bona fide debts heretofore contracted." Shelburne had been afraid that

Jay's phrase might "admit of a quibble," as he phrased it, but the cabinet agreed to it, and it was John Jay, more than any single man, who was to see that this clause was carried out to the letter.[9] Jay never forgot his role in the drafting of this provision and one day as the first chief justice he would uphold the validity of prewar debts guaranteed by the treaty to which his signature was affixed.

Following his successful efforts as a peace commissioner Jay returned home to accept the post of secretary for foreign affairs. It was not long before he realized that Congress' inability to prevent the individual states from obstructing the collection of prewar debts due British creditors constituted an enormous roadblock to harmonious relations with Great Britain. Jay was determined to see that both the federal government and the states carried out to the letter the terms of the treaty with which he was so publicly identified. Long an opponent of uncurbed paper money and an advocate of sound fiscal policy, Jay had now a further ground for opposing the Virginians on this issue.[10]

When, in 1785, John Adams called upon the British government to evacuate the frontier posts which they held in violation of the Treaty of Paris, the Marquess of Carmarthen, the British foreign minister, refused to give them up on the ground that the United States had failed to remove the legal impediments in the way of recovery of debts. In a long report on the British note, submitted to Congress in secret session in October 1786, Jay declared that Great Britain was justified in retaining the posts. One could not blame her for holding on to them while the United States on its side impeded full execution of the treaty, he contended. This report was not made public, but as Samuel Flagg Bemis has elsewhere pointed out, Jay confidentially divulged its nature to Sir John Temple, the British consul at New York.

Bowing to Jay's demands, Congress passed a resolution calling upon the states to remove such obstacles and submitting a copy thereof to each state. Accompanying the congressional resolution was a circular letter composed by Jay, wherein he pointed out the impolicy and bad faith inhering in a failure to execute treaty engagements "constitutionally and fairly made" by the Confederation, and the inconvenience and absurdity of subjecting their terms to the varying interpretations of the legislatures of the thirteen separate states.[11]

The resolution of Congress was honored in the breach, notably by the state of Virginia. In the main Virginia's creditors had been able to put off the evil day, protected as they were by a state law and by the state courts, but the ratification of the Constitution brought dismay to the entire congregation of debtors. St. George Tucker of Virginia wrote to his stepsons, one of them John Randolph of Roanoke: "You will have heard that the Constitution has been adopted in this State. That event, my dear children, affects your interest more nearly than that of many others. The recovery of the British debts can no longer be postponed, and there now seems to be a moral certainty that your patrimony will all go to satisfy the unjust debt from your papa to the Hanburys. The consequence, my dear boys, must be obvious to you. Your sole dependence must be on your personal abilities and exertions."[12] Immediately before Virginia ratified the Constitution, Madison wrote Jefferson that the only opposition he foresaw might come from "ill-timed or rigorous execution of the Treaty of Peace against British debtors."[13]

The "ill-timed" execution of the treaty which Madison feared occurred only too soon. British merchants, long stymied by local state laws and courts, and panting for their pound of flesh, soon deluged the United States circuit courts as well as the Virginia state courts with lawsuits. John Jay as chief justice regarded his charges to the grand jury as an opportunity to expound the constitutional principles upon which the new nation had been founded. Opening the first federal court in New York on April 4, 1790, Jay charged the grand jury on the sanctity of treaties. He described them as obligations upon nations that no state could alter. When he visited states in which debt delinquency was conspicuous he made a special point of repeating these admonitions. He so charged the grand jury in Connecticut on April 22, in Massachusetts on May 4, and in New Hampshire on May 20.[14] So far at least as the Chief Justice was concerned, debtors were placed on notice.

If any doubt remained about the attitude of John Jay and his colleagues toward the obligation of contracts and the liability of debtors to satisfy their creditors in full, it was quickly dissipated in New England, specifically in Rhode Island, where credit–debtor relations had been highly critical in postwar years. Sitting in the circuit for the District of Rhode Island, the Chief Justice handed down a ruling in an unreported case which the files of that court still preserve. This was the lawsuit of *Alexander Champion and Thomas Dickason* v. *Silas Case*. The suit turned upon an act of the Rhode Island General Assembly passed in February 1791, in response to a petition of a debtor for an extension of three years' time in which to settle his accounts with his creditors and for an exemption from all arrests and attachments for such term. The court invalidated the statute on the ground that it conflicted with the obligation of contracts clause of the Constitution.[15] Unlike Georgia's legislature, which reacted violently to *Chisholm* v. *Georgia*, the legislature of Rhode Island meekly concurred in this decision, putting itself on record with the declaration that "they would not grant to any individual an exemption from arrests and attachments for his private debts, for any term of time." Similar decisions handed down between 1793 and 1799, upholding the obligation of contracts clause and invalidating statutes in Connecticut, Pennsylvania, and Vermont, met no serious opposition. As Charles Warren has noted, "no claim was ever then advanced that their action was without constitutional authority." [16]

The storm over the collection of debts in Virginia, on the other hand, proved to be more than a tempest in a teapot. Unlike the Rhode Island situation, it did not involve American creditors seeking to invalidate moratory legislation protecting resident debtors. Instead, it concerned collection by English and Scottish merchants and factors of debts contracted largely before the Revolution. The issue was understandably overlaid with intense political overtones.

The docket of the district of the Virginia circuit was crowded with suits brought by British creditors against their American debtors—cases covered by the provisions of the treaty. Isaac S. Harrell, in his significant study of *Loyalism in Virginia,* found that seventy-five per cent of the cases in Order Book I of the United States Circuit Court of Virginia, covering the period 1790 to 1795, involved contracts between British merchants and American debtors, and that almost every British house trading in Virginia in 1775 was represented. Two suits were entered against Thomas Jefferson as executor and another was entered to recover debts due from the Randolph heirs. The Virginia assembly was moved to action by what seemed the probable outcome of these suits. In November 1791, a week before the circuit court was convened in Virginia, resolutions were introduced in the legislature protesting the recovery . of debts by British subjects until the British had evacuated the western posts and paid for the Negroes carried away during the war. These resolutions failed, however, and the assembly settled for a milder resolution addressed to their senators, urging Congress to come to the relief of Virginia. Congress did nothing.

One of the earliest of the British debt cases to be argued in Virginia, *Jones* v. *Walker,* came up in the circuit at Richmond on November 23, 1791. Jones, representing the Bristol firm of Jones and Farrell, had brought suit against Dr. Thomas Walker of Albemarle County for £2,151 allegedly owing them. Walker's defense was that he had paid the debt into the Virginia loan office on May 25, 1779, in accordance with the provisions of the Virginia law of 1777, and had thereby discharged the debt. The debtors, making common cause with the defendant, employed the famous orator and patriot Patrick Henry, James Innis, the retiring attorney general, John Marshall, a young lawyer soon to make a conspicuous mark on the constitutional law of his country, and Alexander Campbell. Justices Johnson and Blair of the United States Supreme Court and Justice Griffin of the Virginia district court sat on the bench. The feeling was intense, the courtroom was packed, and the judges permitted the vacant seats of the bench and the windows behind it to be occupied.

The decision went on points of law, and there was no jury. The plaintiff argued that debts due to individuals were not subject to confiscation in time of war. Even did such power to confiscate exist, it could be employed only by a sovereign state, and Virginia was not sovereign until Great Britain recognized American independence. The plaintiff further argued that, whether or not the law of Virginia sequestering debts was valid, the debts in question were restored by the treaty of 1783.

Patrick Henry's reply spanned three days. He ridiculed the plaintiff's contention that Virginia was not an independent state "before the monarch of that little island in the

Atlantic gave his puny assent to it." The debts were forfeited and could only be recovered by treaty. However, he
contended, the treaty of 1783 would not provide recovery
since the British had broken that treaty by their refusal to
evacuate the western posts and to pay for the Negroes carried away upon the evacuation of New York. Even if Great
Britain had not broken the treaty, Henry pointed out that
the treaty covered bona fide debts, and that, by paying the
sum at issue into the Virginia loan office in accordance
with Virginia law, the debtor had discharged his debt. The
latter argument was a moot point, and Judges Johnson and
Griffin could not make up their collective mind, while
Justice Blair was called home on account of the death of
his son.[17] Nothing was decided, and the issue still remained
in suspense.[18]

The argument over the British debts begun in *Jones v.
Walker* in November was again advanced in the notable
case of *Ware, Administrator of Jones, v. Hylton*. By the
time the case came up in May term of 1793, before Chief
Justice Jay, and Judges Iredell and Griffin, the plaintiff
Jones had died, and the Court had permitted his administrator, Ware, to reopen the case.[19] Jay, and surely not by
coincidence, had once again publicly spelled out his position. In a charge to the grand jury at Richmond at the opening of the circuit on May 22, Jay adverted to the subject of
treaties and conformity to obligations.

Nations no less than individuals, Jay instructed the
Grand Jury, "injure their essential interests in proportion
as they deviate from order." He defined order as "that national regularity which results from attention and obedience to those rules and principles of conduct which reason
indicates and which morality and wisdom prescribe." Com-
prehended within these rules were the laws of the land,
consisting of "the Constitution, the statutes of Congress,

the laws of nations, and treaties constitutionally made." These rules, he described as having a twofold objective, the regulation of the conduct of our own citizens relative to "our own nation and people," and the regulation of that conduct "relative to foreign nations and their subjects." In the first category he put statutes concerning commerce, navigation, and finance, and notably those respecting revenue. The object of the latter was, as Jay saw it, "to provide for the payment of debts already accrued, and to provide for the *current* and for the *contingent* expenses of the government and nation."

Having come to the sensitive subject of debts, an especially touchy topic in the city of Richmond, Jay declared that both justice and policy dictated that "debts fairly contracted should be honestly paid." Speaking in Hamiltonian language, he asserted that only on this basis "can public credit be erected and supported." Those who regard "fraud and chicane" as a "justifiable or useful instrument of policy," he denounced as either wanting in "wisdom or virtue, or both." This comment must be borne in mind when we consider one of the choices that Jay as statesman and politician faced as governor of New York. Excoriating the man or nation who evaded the payment of debts as unworthy of further credit, he added in his original draft in the Jay Papers: "We are all interested in the Honor and advantage of public credit—and therefore it is proper that all should unite in defending and maintaining it." Our credit, he reminded the grand jury, would always be proportionate "to our resources, to our integrity, and to our punctuality." Since all citizens had an interest in the public credit, it was the duty of the grand jury to inquire into and present such violations of the revenue laws as they might find to have been committed within their district.

Aside from federal law, the grand jury's attention was

directed to the laws of nations. "It is much to be wished" that the subject of the laws of nations "may be more generally studied and understood," Jay observed. Who made the laws of nations? he asked. "The answer is *he* from whose *will* proceed *all* moral obligations, and which *will* is made known to us by reason or by revelation." Jay, it must be remembered, was a devoutly religious person, holding more orthodox views on the subject of revealed religion than many of the other Founding Fathers.

Cautioning the grand jurors about the need to maintain strict neutrality in accordance with the national policy in the current war between France and England, he instructed the grand jury to present persons engaged in fitting out privateers, recruiting for a foreign power, or any foreigners committing seditious or hostile acts against the United States.

Jay anticipated the argument of defendant debtors that America was justified in disregarding its provisions concerning the debts and the Tories since Britain had violated the treaty of 1783. Thus, in his original draft Jay stated: "Every treaty observed by both parties is binding on both, neither party by violating it can absolve himself from the obligation of it, but the other party against whom the violation is committed may or may not take advantage of that violation and either disannul the treaty or make reprisals or demand and accept reparation as may best suit his interest. You will perceive therefore that the annulling of treaties by reason of infractions is a political one." It involved political considerations. Should we remonstrate? Should we demand reparation? Should we direct reprisals? Are we ready for war, or should we avoid running that risk until we can be better prepared for it? "These and a variety of similar considerations ought to precede and govern the decision of those who annul violated treaties, order reprisals, or declare war." Meanwhile the nation must either move together or "lose its force." We must preserve peace until war is declared. As free citizens we have a right to speak our sentiments on this subject "in terms becoming freemen," but as judges and grand jurors "the merits of those questions are without our province." In sum, the Chief Justice charged the grand jury that until the United States had annulled the treaty of 1783, taken steps to demand reparations, or gone to war, it was the duty of the citizens to obey it.

This was strong language indeed in the city of Richmond, where pro-French sentiment ran high and debtors clamored for relief against their detested British creditors. In this atmosphere the case of *Ware* v. *Hylton* was heard in May 1793, coming up before Chief Justice Jay and Judges Iredell and Griffin immediately after Jay's charge to the grand jury. The British creditors engaged a leader of the Virginia bar, John Wickham, who had followed a neutralist course in the war. Opposing him, of course, was Patrick Henry, that stalwart champion of all debtor patriots. "Your countrymen look up to you as their rock of salvation," the defendant Daniel L. Hylton wrote to Henry when he engaged him.[20] Before the lower court Henry spoke with his usual eloquence, but his arguments were emotional rather than founded on reason and the technicalities of the law. Moved though he was by Henry's eloquence, Iredell confessed that "in the course of many points he has argued he has not satisfied me in the slightest degree as to anything but the payments into the treasury."[21]

Since the case in the lower court has never been either fully or accurately reported, our knowledge of it comes from garbled versions in contemporary letters and the press. However, from the Court's order book and record book, still in manuscript form in Richmond, it is possible to reconstruct the split decision. Through an interminable course of pleas, replications, rejoinders, and demurrers, it appears that the defense rested its case on two basic points: first, that the payment to the loan office for which a receipt signed by Thomas Jefferson was offered in evidence barred recovery under the act of 1777; secondly, that since the debts were originally due to British subjects, who after July 4, 1776, were enemies at war, they were not recoverable in court. To these pleas the plaintiff demurred, citing the pertinent article in the treaty of 1783, to which in rejoinder the defendant pleaded a prior breach of that treaty by the British.

As regards the first plea, the majority of the court, Jay dissenting, held that the payment to the loan office covered that portion of the debt represented by the face amount of the certificate, but as to the second plea the Court unanimously upheld the plaintiff. The following year, a jury handed down a verdict of $596 in damages with interest at five per cent since July 7, 1782, along with court costs. Thus the court had really straddled the issue. It upheld the legality of the Virginia law by which debtors of British creditors could secure relief from their obligations while at the same time it refused to accept the defendant's plea that the treaty of 1783 was not controlling. That it took the latter stand must be credited in no small measure to Jay's public charge to the grand jury on the issue of the enforcement of treaties.

Jay's dissenting opinion, if it actually was rendered as a formal opinion, unfortunately has not survived, nor is it recorded in either the order or the record book. One newspaper correspondent called it "one of the most able opinions I ever heard delivered—and to disinterested persons the most satisfactory and conclusive." But it was Iredell's majority opinion that was read into the record of the case when it reached the Supreme Court. Justice Iredell's pithy account of the case is worth noting. In a letter to his wife dated June 7, 1793, he wrote: "We have this day given judgment on the great question as to British causes which has been depending so long. The judgment was in favor of the plaintiff, but with the exception of certain sums paid into the Treasury. Mr. Griffin and myself concurred. Mr. Jay was for overruling it." [22]

Ware v. *Hylton*, coming as it did at the height of political agitation in America between Federalists and anti-Federalists over support for the French Revolution, showed Jay to be both a man of courage and a stickler for the full letter of the law. "No enemy to the French Revolution," wrote one correspondent from Richmond, as quoted in the *National Gazette* for July 3, 1793, "dares open his mouth." Jay's stand, it need hardly be pointed out, was acutely unpopular in Virginia. Edmund Randolph, then attorney general of the United States, reported to President Washington from Virginia that the Chief Justice reputedly had been insulted by a drunken man who was present at the trial in the circuit court. [23] The Virginia assembly instructed their senators to move in Congress that the fourth article of the treaty of 1783 (the article providing for the payment of debts) be suspended until the United States should have assurances that the treaty was being fulfilled by Great Britain. On May 6, 1794, Senator James Monroe, later the fifth President of the United States, moved to bring in such a bill and was supported by the radical exponent of agrarianism, John Taylor of Caroline. Monroe succeeded only in getting Taylor's vote, however, for fourteen other senators voted against the motion, and it went down to defeat. [24] The issue did not quiet down in Virginia. In August 1794, the grand jury of the federal circuit of Virginia presented "as a *national* grievance the recovery of debts due to British subjects, contracted prior to the year 1774." The action of the Virginia grand jury elicited this unsympathetic reaction from a Yankee newspaper. "Spendall in the play says, 'It is a cursed thing to pay debts—it has ruined many a man.' " [25]

That part of the majority decision of the Virginia Circuit Court in *Ware* v. *Hylton* which had ruled that debtors were no longer liable for sums paid into the state loan office under the laws of Virginia was re-argued upon appeal in the United States Supreme Court at Philadelphia in February 1796. This time the creditors were represented by Edward Tilghman, Alexander Willcocks, and William Lewis of Philadelphia, while for the defendant appeared John Marshall and Alexander Campbell, both of whom had been associated with Patrick Henry for the defense in the district court. It is John Marshall's appearance and his line of argument that reveals the difference between the opinions of the advocate and the statesman. In the former role Marshall put up the best defense possible for his client, even though he assuredly was not convinced of its merits himself. Arguing against the binding force of the treaty over state legislation, the future chief justice referred to "those who wish to impair the sovereignty of Virginia," using, as Charles Warren remarked, "the very phrase which the ardent States' Rights adherents used so frequently in after years in attacking his own decisions as Chief Justice." In any event, despite his arguments, he was wined and dined by the Federalists who knew that here was a man who supported the national government, even though a Virginian, "such a *rara avis,*" Marshall so described himself, "that I was received with a degree of kindness which I had not anticipated." [26]

Marshall had made a strong personal impression, but his arguments failed to convince the Court. In the interval between the trial on the circuit and the appeal before the

Supreme Court, John Jay had resigned as chief justice to accept the governorship of New York state; but the four judges then sitting on the appeal (Paterson, Cushing, Wilson, and Chase) unanimously upheld his dissenting view and in the notable opinion, written by Justice Chase, declared that the British treaty provisions must prevail over state laws, that the treaty had removed the legal impediments to recovery, and that so far as it is compatible with the Constitution a treaty supersedes all state laws which derogate from its provisions. Thereby the Supreme Court settled forever one of the fundamental questions of American constitutional law.[27]

The practical consequence of this decision was that a sum in excess of a quarter of a million pounds that had been paid into the loan office to discharge the debts had to be paid again, this time to the creditors. Quite naturally, the debtors looked to Virginia for relief, and the House of Delegates was deluged with petitions from debtors of British merchants. In turn the delegates instructed the senators from Virginia to obtain compensation for the citizen debtors. Although the money which had been paid into the loan office had presumably been used by Virginia to carry on the war and might be considered as belonging to that class of state debts assumed by the federal government, the national government gave the state no aid; it was left for the Virginia legislature itself to vote for the issue of interest-bearing certificates payable to the debtors who had made payments. In passing it should also be noted that Chancellor Wythe, Virginia's pre-eminent jurist, also ruled in the Virginia state court that the payments into the loan office of Virginia did not discharge debts due to British subjects, thereby paying obeisance to Jay's dissent in *Ware* v. *Hylton*.[28]

These affirmative decisions in both federal and state

courts did not resolve the issue of the British debts. In the first place, the federal courts had no jurisdiction over debts under five hundred dollars, and a great number of the debts fell into this category. One observer put the majority of debts as under a hundred dollars.[29] The debtors continued to use one device after another in a vain effort to bar recovery; but they did succeed in winning a ruling from the Virginia courts barring interest on debts during the period of the war.[30] The issue of the British debts was still unsettled when in 1794 John Jay repaired to the Court of St. James on his controversial diplomatic mission to settle the grievances outstanding between England and the United States.

In agreeing to undertake this diplomatic assignment, the Chief Justice was not consistent with his earlier public position. The Jay court, it should be recalled, had at the start entertained strict views of its functions and carefully eschewed political or administrative tasks. Save for his grand jury charges with their heavy political overtones, Jay, although continuing privately to counsel the other branches of the government, had kept his court from taking on political or administrative tasks. (There was one exception. Two years before the Jay mission to England, the Chief Justice had waged a campaign for the governorship of New York and acceded without rancor to the results of a palpably fraudulent election count which awarded that contest to the durable George Clinton.) A justice of the Supreme Court can hardly serve on a controversial diplomatic mission without bringing the Court into politics or raising the implication that somehow such presidential nominations for extrajudicial duties constitute a reward for conduct on the bench.

Yet neither Washington nor Jay thought about this assignment as other than a patriotic obligation. "No appointment ever operated more unpleasantly upon me," Jay wrote his wife, "but the public considerations which were urged and the manner in which it was pressed, strongly impressed me with a conviction that to refuse it would be, to desert my duty for the sake of my ease and domestic concerns and comforts." [31] In placing his duty to serve the cause of peace and better Anglo–American relations ahead of his judicial responsibilities, the Chief Justice did what may have been right for him. At the same time his diplomatic involvement exposed him to sharp criticism and might have been utilized by others as a precedent for overstepping the separation of powers. Fortunately, only in a relatively few instances have Supreme Court justices taken on nonjudicial duties, whether acting as a prosecutor at a war-crimes trial or presiding over a commission of inquiry concerning a presidential assassination. The exceptions only serve to reinforce the rule. The Court has in the main prudently avoided nonjudicial chores.

Jay was cordially welcomed by court circles because he was believed to be favorably disposed toward England or at least sympathetic to conciliation. He showed that he had not changed his mind since 1785, when as secretary for foreign affairs, he had enunciated his original views about treaty infractions. He was not moved by Jefferson's argument that the failure of the British to evacuate the posts had preceded and thereby provoked American legal impediments to recovery of debts. He found more compelling the argument of his diplomatic counterpart, Lord Grenville, the British foreign minister, that no orders for evacuation need have been given by the British until the proclamation of formal ratification of the treaty had been received in Canada in July 1784. Therefore, since the state legislatures had passed in the interval various laws barring recovery, Jay was inclined to accept the argument that America's treaty infractions predated those charged to the British. Reinforcing this new line was Jay's well-known views of debtors who sought to evade their obligations by hiding behind the protection of state laws.

Jay now proposed to Grenville (and the latter agreed) that the United States make compensation for debts, the recovery of which may have been prevented by legal impediments, and that a mixed commission sitting in the United States should decide on these claims, which the United States was to pay in specie. What is notable, even startling about the stipulation as it was finally incorporated into the treaty that bears Jay's name, is that it provides for appeals from the American courts to the joint commission. When "strict legal evidence"—because of lapse of time or impediments to recovery—did not exist, claimants could petition the commission, presenting any kind of evidence, which the commissioners should "judge equitably and impartially, according to the circumstances." This included ex parte evidence from factor's accounts, inadmissible at common law. Payment for all debts validated by the commission were to be assumed by the United States. The article on the debts in the draft treaty did not stipulate a guaranty of interest for the war years, but left to the mixed commission, ruling by majority vote (it eventually proved to be a majority of three English commissioners against two Americans) judgment of all claims "whether of principal or interest."

Jay has been sharply rebuked for not upholding the honor of a judicial court over which he presided at home. His critics maintain that he ought to have insisted on the Court's competence to interpret the treaty and on the sufficiency of its justice. By failing to do so he made it possible for British claimants to circumvent the American courts and to utilize a procedure which would expedite their claims. The claims of the American creditors, on the other hand, were held up, because those with claims *against* British citizens were required to run the gamut of the British judicial system before a mixed commission sitting in London would entertain their suits.

Admittedly these criticisms have some justification, and one wonders why the Chief Justice stripped his own court of jurisdiction over cases which it had shown itself competent to rule upon with impartiality. On the credit side, praise is due Jay for his notable innovation in international law, the principle of mixed commissions, which the United States and Great Britain subsequently used in the settlement of their disputes. Jay had drawn the notion from the New York–New Jersey Boundary Commission, which he had served as secretary when a young attorney. With that colonial experience in mind, Jay provided in his treaty for the appointment of a joint commission to hear claims arising under the treaty of 1783; two of its members were to be named by the United States, two by Great Britain, and a fifth member was to be selected by the appointed commissioners. As it worked out the four commissioners selected the fifth member by lot, and the choice fell upon the British nominee. As a result, the British secured a majority on the commission. A deadlock ensued. The British insisted that interest on the debts should be paid for the period during the war; the Americans dissented. The British likewise urged the restoration of the estates of Loyalists confiscated by bills of attainder; again the Americans refused to agree. After considerable discussion, the Americans withdrew from the commission, and the negotiations were stopped.

Jefferson's election in 1800, signalizing a victory of the agrarian over the commercial classes, gave Virginians renewed authority in the councils of government. It is hardly a coincidence that the dispute with Great Britain over the debts should then be settled by the compromise formula adopted by the Convention of 1802. In this convention, the United States agreed to pay six hundred thousand pounds sterling to the British government in settlement of all outstanding claims, an amount that was duly paid from the treasury of the United States in three annual installments.[32] This was in fact less than a third of what the committee of British merchants had demanded of Grenville.

The issue of the debts is long since settled. The credit of the United States was restored in large measure by Hamilton's bold financial program, but Jay's extraordinary efforts as jurist and diplomat made a substantial contribution too. The British poured huge capital investments into America, a fund of credit which promoted American public works, contributed to the expansion of commerce and industry, to public improvements, roads, canals, and the railroads. Without that credit America's expansion and industrialization would have been held back at least a generation. It is perhaps idle to speculate on just how critically the economic growth of the new nation would have been curbed had it not been for Hamilton's sound financial program and Jay's insistence that the nation enforce the obligation of contracts.

More important than pounds or dollars, even transcending the issues of both private and public morality which were involved, was the notion of the supremacy of treaties. For more than a dozen years after the treaty of peace, state legislatures and individuals had sought to circumvent the treaty by stay laws, paper money and legal tender laws, acts confiscating Tory property, and similar retaliatory and vengeful measures. The reputation of America as a new nation had been seriously impaired. Jay's stand in behalf of the enforcement of treaties was not only a powerful stroke for national supremacy within the nation but also for upholding the nation's reputation in the rest of the world. For the young and untried republic to win equal standing among the states of a largely hostile world, it was essential that it provide a solid demonstration that it respected treaties and gave them the same standing as the fundamental charter of the land, the United States Constitution.

Critics of Jay's final settlement of the debt issue have charged that the Chief Justice, in turning the settlement over to a mixed commission, damaged the prestige and authority of his own court. When one reflects on the hostility with which the nation reacted to *Chisholm* v. *Georgia,* it might well appear that Jay demonstrated prudence and common sense in keeping this emotionally charged political issue from further undermining the authority of the Court. If Jay's diplomacy led to some dilution of federal jurisdiction, it may be added that he more than made amends in the last decision in which he participated, the case of *Glass* v. *Betsey,* decided at the February Term, 1794.[33]

Speaking for the Court, and reversing the decision of the district court of Maryland, Jay asserted the full power of the United States District Court, under its admiralty jurisdiction, to determine the legality of prize ships brought into ports of the United States by foreign, in this instance, French, privateers. In accordance with his stand at the time of the negotiations over the consular convention with France, he denied the right of any foreign nation, in the absence of treaty stipulation, to establish a court for the exercise of such jurisdiction within the territory of the United States. Jay thereby upheld the complete national sovereignty of the United States over violations of international law in that field. Commenting on this opinion, Charles Warren has observed that "no decision of the Court ever did more to vindicate our international rights, to establish respect amongst other nations for the sovereignty of this country, and to keep the United States out of international complications." [34]

Only a short time later Jay spelled out the Supreme Court's jurisdiction over foreign consuls. That same year at the April session of the circuit court for the Pennsylvania district Jay upheld the power of the federal court to punish a consul from Genoa named Joseph Ravara, who had been indicted for sending threatening letters to George Hammond, the British minister to the United States. Jay held that Ravara was not privileged from prosecution by virtue of his consular appointment. In a significant and hitherto unpublished retrospective minority opinion in this case Jay considered whether the Constitution gave the Supreme Court jurisdiction over foreign consuls. When the case had come before an earlier sitting of the circuit court, Judges Wilson and Peters, in a majority opinion, had ruled that the Judiciary Act gave concurrent jurisdiction to the circuit court in such cases. Jay had denied that the act did explicitly confer such jurisdiction upon the circuit court, and in words which were prophetic of *Marbury* v. *Madison*, remarked that if Congress "had, and either in this instance or any other had made a provision inconsistent with the Constitution, the latter, *as the supreme law*, must necessarily control the former, although no one could imagine that Congress, though they might in the hurry of business inadvertently make a provision inconsistent with the Constitution, deliberately meant to transgress it." [35]

Jay devoted his brief tenure on the bench to expounding the Constitution as a nationalist chief justice might have been expected to interpret it and to enforcing the nation's treaty obligations. He was active neither as a court reformer nor as an expositor of technical branches of law. Antagonistic as he was to the tasks of circuit riding imposed on the Supreme Court justices, he advised President Washington to avoid "fierce" divisions by refraining from making concrete proposals for the revision of the judicial system. He recognized, as he remarked to Rufus King, that "the federal courts have enemies in all who fear their influence on state objects," and he was concerned lest by exposing to public view these defects in all their "striking colors . . . more enemies would arise," thereby compounding the difficulties of reform. Accordingly, substantial revisions were deferred until 1801.[36]

Jay was no technician of the law, and some of his controversial opinions carried scant legal research to bolster them. The view of his court that Congress could enlarge the original jurisdiction of the Supreme Court was repudiated by later courts, which confined its original jurisdiction to the cases enumerated in the Constitution.[37] Jay assumed an even more controversial stance when he asserted the existence of a federal common law of crime by which, independently of acts of Congress, the courts could punish offenses against the laws of nations or administrative regulations concerning neutrality. Jay expounded this doctrine to a grand jury impaneled in Richmond in May 1793. A few months later Judge Wilson incorporated the idea into his charge to the jury in the trial of Gideon Henfield, charged with engaging in privateering operations for France. Although Henfield was acquitted by a jury responsive to popular clamor against the prosecution, the circuit court for the Pennsylvania district two years later upheld the power of the United States courts to try a person indicted on a common-law crime. In *United States* v. *Ravara,* Justices Jay and Peters held that the offense of the Genoese consul, though not a crime by state or federal statute, was indictable at common law.[38] Not long after, and before the passage of the Sedition Act, the federal courts discovered a common law of seditious libel. Both Republican and Federalist editors in turn felt the sting of this harsh, imprecise, and mischievous doctrine, which was overturned, so far as a federal common law of crime is concerned, in 1812.[39] Aside from crimes, the doctrine that there was a federal common law was elaborated upon by Justice Story in 1842. It was finally jettisoned in 1938.[40]

The Chief Justice has been criticized for enlarging the scope of the jury and permitting it to judge both the law and the facts. Jay cited no authorities in support of his position, but as Associate Justice Black has only recently pointed out in a dissenting opinion, the law was extremely cloudy on this point in Jay's time, and views similar to Jay's were expounded in a number of state courts as well as by Associate Justice Wilson in the course of his law lectures at the College of Philadelphia.[41]

In sum, while Jay's opinions on points of law have not stood the test of time in some cases, his audaciously nationalistic exposition of the Constitution has been reaffirmed and applied in areas beyond the purview of the Founding Fathers. By character, training, and experience, he was peculiarly fitted to occupy the posts of responsibility and decision-making that he filled during a period when the national government needed energetic and bold direction and an outlook that was continental rather than provincial. One is impelled to compare his political and constitutional ideas with those of Hamilton. Similarities there are, certainly, between the constitutional views of Alexander Hamilton and those of John Jay; but these should not blind us to the equally significant differences in their methods, tone, and style; these differences reflect fundamental contrasts in personality and character. Nothing brings these basic differences into sharper relief than the behavior of John Jay during the election of 1800.

In the spring of that year the Jeffersonian Democratic-Republicans had won control of the New York legislature, which soon would cast its electoral votes for the presidency. Since New York's twelve electoral votes would automatically go to Jefferson and Burr, the election of the Democratic-

Republican candidates to the two top posts in the land seemed assured. Hamilton, who by his unprincipled and unrestrained attack on President John Adams during the election campaign, had reached his nadir as a politician, now urged Jay to call back the adjourned Federalist legislature into special session and have it pass an act for redistricting the state and choosing presidential electors by popular ballot. Had Jay done so, the Federalists might have picked up five and possibly six of the electors—enough to elect a Federalist president. On May 7, 1800, Hamilton put this devious proposal to Jay in writing. "In times like these in which we live, it will not do to be overscrupulous," Hamilton wrote. Finding reasons to satisfy himself that his proposal was morally justified, Hamilton argued that this was an extraordinary crisis, one in which the usual delicacy and propriety "ought not to hinder the taking of a legal and constitutional step, to prevent an atheist in religion and a fanatic in politics from getting possession of the helm of state."

If Hamilton lost his head, Jay did not. He did not agree with Hamilton's arguments. He felt that the will of the people had been expressed in the April elections which had returned a Democratic–Republican legislature. Was it fair to change the rules in the middle of the game? Taking up Hamilton's letter, he turned it over and thus endorsed it: "Proposing a measure for *party* purposes, which I think it would not become me to adopt." The decision assured Jefferson his election, and thereby altered the course of American history. It was in character for Jay to permit his party to go down to defeat rather than to win dishonorably.

In retrospect, Jay's contribution to the Supreme Court in its formative years takes on large dimensions despite the paucity of business which came before that tribunal in its early days, his relatively brief tenure as chief justice, and the suspicion with which the Court was regarded by large segments of the nation. In view of Jay's previous record, one might have expected him to leave his mark as a technician of the law. Instead, he is remembered as a creative statesman and activist chief justice whose concepts of the broad purpose and powers of the new nation under the Constitution were to be upheld and spelled out with boldness and vigor by John Marshall. In bringing the states into subordination to the federal government, in securing from both the states and the people reluctant recognition of the supremacy of treaties, and in laying the foundation for the later exercise by the Supreme Court of the power to declare acts of Congress unconstitutional, Jay gave bold directions to the new constitutional regime. His tireless effort to endow the national government with energy, capacity, and scope and to assert the authority of the people over that of the states attest to his vision, courage, and tenacity. It remained for others to spell out the safeguards for individual liberties and the limitation on national power which are so essential to the maintenance of a democratic society. As a humanitarian and civil libertarian, John Jay, the patrician, could take pardonable pride in the result.

NOTES

Chapter I. The Wellsprings of Jay's Nationalism

1. Peter Jay to Sir James, April 14, 1763; Letterbooks, Jay Papers, Special Collections, Columbia University Libraries (hereinafter cited JP); Milton M. Klein, "Prelude to Revolution in New York: Jury Trials and Judicial Tenure," *William and Mary Quarterly*, 3rd ser., XVII:439–462.

2. This was the case of Forsey *v.* Cunningham, in which the Privy Council, after first permitting an appeal, reversed itself in late December 1765, and denied the right of appeal. See *ibid*; Joseph H. Smith, *Appeals to the Privy Council from the American Plantations* (New York, 1950), pp. 390–416.

3. See R. B. Morris, "Legalism versus Revolutionary Doctrine in New England," *New England Quarterly*, IV:195–215.

4. Benjamin Kissam to John Jay, August 25, 1766, JP; Notes on July Assizes, 1766, New York Historical Society; Irving Mark and Oscar Handlin, "Land Cases in Colonial New York, 1765–1767: The King *v.* William Prendergast," *New York University Law Quarterly Review*, XIX:194 (1942). On John Jay as a lawyer, see Herbert Johnson, "The Legal Career of John Jay" (unpub. Ph.D. diss., Columbia University, 1965).

5. This was the case of King *v.* Underhill, cited by Johnson, "The Legal Career," pp. 157–160.

6. The Supreme Court held that the judgment in debt rendered in Massachusetts had not been proven as a fact, and for this reason the demurrer of the defendant should have been sustained. Bemus *v.* Fellows, appealed from Mayor's Court of Albany on writ of error (May 20, 1770), Albany Mayor's Court Minutes, Albany County Clerk's Office, lib. 1768–1778, p. 65; parchment 136 G-1, Hall of Records, New York; JJ to Peter W. Yates, March 23, 1772, Misc. MSS, Peter W. Yates, New York Historical Society.

7. See Minutes of the Moot, Nov. 23, 1770–May 13, 1774, p. 34, N.Y. Historical Society.

8. See N.Y.–N.J. Boundary Commission Papers, JP; also Johnson, "The Legal Career," pp. 101–107.

9. H. P. Johnston, ed., *Correspondence and Public Papers of John Jay* (New York ,1890–1893), I:17 ff. (hereinafter cited *JPJ*).

10. For a photocopy of the JJ draft see "Olive Branch Petition," July (n.d.) 1775, JP; see also *JPJ*, I:33 *n*.

11. See "Congress and Independence," a paper attributed to JJ (January 1776), *JPJ*, I:52–56.

12. JJ to Alexander McDougall, March 27, 1776, McDougall Papers, N.Y. Historical Society.

13. See Bernard Mason, *The Road to Independence* (Lexington, Ky., 1966), pp. 168–169.

14. "Resolutions of New York Convention Approving the Declaration of Independence," *JPJ*, I:72–73.

15. See JJ to Robert Morris, Oct. 6, 1776, *JPJ*, I:87.

16. *JPJ*, I:113; JJ to John Adams, Aug. 2, 1782, Adams Papers, Massachusetts Historical Society (hereinafter cited AP); *JPJ*, II:324–325.

17. JJ to McDougall, April 11, 1776, N.Y. Historical Society.

18. JJ to James Duane, May 29, 1776, *JPJ*, I:63. Duane, on the other hand, felt that the colony should not be "too precipitate in changing the present mode of Government." Duane to JJ, May 18, 1776, *ibid.*, I:61; JJ to Robert R. Livingston, May 29, 1776, *ibid.*, I:65.

19. *Ibid.*, I:68.

20. "Address of the Mechanicks of New York City to the Delegates of the Congress of New York," Peter Force, *American Archives* (4th ser.; Washington, 1837–1853), VI:895.

21. JJ to Robert R. Livingston, May 29, 1776, *JPJ*, I:65; *Journal of the Provincial Congress*, I:460–462, 463.

22. *Ibid.*, I:526–527, 552, 568, 821, 823, 825, 833.

23. For the attribution of Draft "A" to Jay, see Nathaniel H. Carter and William L. Stone, *Reports of the Proceedings and Debates of the Convention of 1821* (Albany, 1821), Appendix, p. 692. For the view that the fifth and final draft was Jay's handiwork, see *N.Y. Columbian*, June 16, 19, 1821, reprinted in *ibid.*, p. 692. For the most recent review of the evidence, see Mason, *Road to Independence*, pp. 225–229.

24. JJ to Robert R. Livingston and Gouverneur Morris, April 29, 1777, Bancroft America Series, I:218–21, copy in the New York Public Library; *JPJ*, I:128–130.

25. Amendments of March 21, 26, and April 1, 1777, in *Journals of the Provincial Congress, Provincial Convention, Commit-*

tee of Safety, 1775–1777 (Albany, 1842), I:846, 852, 860. The constitution is reprinted in *ibid.*, pp. 890–898.

26. *Calendar of Historical Manuscripts Relative to the War of the Revolution in the Office of the Secretary of State* (2 vols.; Albany, 1868).

27. Charles Z. Lincoln, *The Constitutional History of New York* (Rochester, 1906), I:515. For a recent appraisal of Jay's views on democracy, see David H. Fischer, *The Revolution of American Conservatism* (New York, 1965), pp. 7–10.

28. JJ to Robert R. Livingston and Gouverneur Morris, April 29, 1777, *JPJ*, I:135–136.

29. JJ to Abraham Yates, May 16, 1777, *ibid.*, I:137.

30. JJ to Leonard Gansevoort, June 5, 1777, *ibid.*, I:141.

31. Jay's charge to the Grand Jury of Ulster County, *ibid.*, I:158–165.

32. Lincoln, *Constitutional History*, I:577–581.

33. See R. B. Morris, *The Peacemakers* (New York, 1965), p. 312.

34. John Adams to JJ, Paris, May 13, 1780, JP.

35. JJ to Franklin, March 18, 1782, JP.

36. JA to Elbridge Gerry, Dec. 14, 1782, Adams Papers Microfilm.

37. JJ to Egbert Benson, Paris, Aug. 26, 1782, JP.

38. JJ to Washington, Paris, April 6, 1783, Washington Papers, Library of Congress.

39. JJ to William Livingston, Passy, July 19, 1783, JP.

40. Quoted in *The Peacemakers*, pp. 458–459.

41. JJ to William Bingham, Passy, July 29, 1783, JP.

42. See JJ to Philip Schuyler, Sept. 16, 1783 to Feb. 19, 1784, JP; Julian P. Boyd, *Number 7: Alexander Hamilton's Secret Attempts to Control American Foreign Policy* (Princeton, N.J., 1964), pp. x, xi.

43. Adams to Jay, June 26, 1785, Papers of the Continental Congress (hereinafter cited PCC), item 84, National Archives, V:522–527. See also R. B. Morris, "The Confederation Period and the American Historian," *William and Mary Quarterly*, 3rd ser., XIII:139–156.

44. JJ, Report to Congress, Feb. 16, 1785, PCC, item 124, Transcripts of Reports of JJ, 1785–1789, pp. 16–21; item 81, Reports of JJ, 1785–1788, National Archives, I–III:7–21.

45. JJ, Report to Congress, May 13, 1785, PCC, item 124, pp. 77–79; item 81, Reports of JJ, 1785–1788, National Archives, I–III:219–221.

46. S. F. Bemis, ed. *The American Secretaries of State and Their Diplomacy* (New York, 1927), I:251–257. See also JJ, Report to Congress, Jan. 10, 1787, PCC, item 81, Reports of JJ, 1785–1788, I–III:173–179. For JJ's opposition to employing citizens of other lands as U.S. consuls, see Report of Congress, Jan. 10, 1787, PCC.

47. See also *JPJ*, III:199, 222–223; JJ, Report to Congress, Aug. 2, 1787, PCC, item 81, Reports of JJ, 1785–1788, Vols I–III:139–142.

48. Bemis, *American Secretaries of State*, I:271.

49. JJ to Thomas Jefferson, Aug. 18, 1786 (draft), JP; J. P. Boyd, ed., *The Papers of Thomas Jefferson* (Princeton, N.J., 1950–1965), X:271, 272.

50. JJ to Washington, Jan. 7, 1787, Washington Papers, Library of Congress.

51. JJ to John Lowell, May 10, 1785 in George Pellew, *John Jay* (Boston, New York, 1894), p. 249; taken by Pellew from William Jay, *The Life of John Jay* (New York, 1833), I:190.

52. JJ to Edward Rutledge, Dec. 12, 1786 (abstract), JP.

53. JJ to George Read, Dec. 12, 1786, Morristown National Historical Park, Morristown, N.J.

54. JJ to William Carmichael, Jan. 4, 1787, JP.

55. JJ to Ferdinand Grand, Dec. 1785, *ibid.*

56. JJ to Washington, March 16, 1786, Washington Papers, Library of Congress.

57. JJ to William Stephens Smith, July 20, 1787, Yale University.

58. *Ibid;* JJ to George Mason, Jr., Aug. 9, 1787 (draft), JP.

59. See the account in Sarah Livingston Jay to Susan F. Livingston, April 17, 1788, *ibid.*

60. Jay's essay No. 2 appeared in the New York *Independent Journal,* Oct. 31, 1787, and in the *Daily Advertiser* and *New York Packet,* November 4 and 5, respectively.

61. Jay also made this point in his debates in the ratifying convention. See Jonathan Elliot, ed., *Debates in the Several State Conventions on the Adoption of the Federal Constitution* (2nd. ed.; Washington, 1836), II:282.

62. Franklin letter in E. W. Spaulding, *New York in the Critical Period, 1783–1789* (New York, 1932), p. 211; George Washington to JJ, May 1788, *JPJ*, III:332.

63. The pamphlet is conveniently reprinted in *ibid.*, III:294–323.

64. JJ to Washington, Feb. 3, 1788 (draft), JP; JJ to Washington, April 12, 1788 (draft), *ibid.*

65. JJ to Washington, May 29, 1788 (draft), *ibid.*

66. This notion is mentioned by JJ to Washington as early as May 29, *ibid.* The groundwork had been laid in Jay's *Address to the People* published the previous month. *JPJ*, III:316–317.

67. JJ to Washington, July 4, 8, 1788, Washington Papers, Library of Congress.

68. For a recent eulogy of Hamilton's role, see Catherine Drinker Bowen, *Miracle at Philadelphia* (Boston, 1966). Hamilton's role is downgraded in Linda G. De Pauw, *The Eleventh Pillar: New York State and the Federal Convention* (Ithaca, 1966), pp. 186–253, *passim.* See also Charles Tillinghast to John Lamb, June 21, 1788, John Lamb Papers, N.Y. Historical Society.

69. June 23, 1788, *Debates and Proceedings of the Constitutional Convention of the State of New York Assembled at Poughkeepsie* (New York, 1905), pp. 57–60; John McKesson, MS, "Notes on the Ratifying Convention," N.Y. Historical Society; June 25, 1788, Elliot, *Debates*, II:325–327.

70. June 30–July 1, 1788, *ibid.*, II:380–381; McKesson, "Notes."

71. July 2, *ibid.*; Melancton Smith, "Notes on the Poughkeepsie Convention," New York State Library.

72. See McKesson, "Notes"; Smith, "Notes." A fresh appraisal of Melancton Smith's role is offered in Robin Brooks, "Alexander Hamilton, Melancton Smith, and the Ratification of the Constitution in New York," *William and Mary Quarterly* (July, 1967).

73. The draft, July 28, 1788, in John McKesson Papers, N.Y. Historical Society, is in JJ's hand, except for the addition beginning "Our Amendments will manifest" to "States with whom we unite," which is in the hand of Robert R. Livingston. See also *Independent Journal* (New York), suppl., July 28, 1788.

74. Jay to Wilberforce, Oct. 25, 1810, *JPJ*, IV:335–338.

Chapter II. Jay, the Supreme Court, and the Subordination of the States

1. Article III, sec. 2, par. 1.

2. Jay, *Life of John Jay*, I:274. This is implied also in Washington to Madison, Aug. 9, 1789, J. C. Fitzpatrick, *Writings of Washington* (Washington, 1939), pp. 30, 374–375.

3. George Washington to JJ, Oct. 5, 1789, *JPJ*, III:378.

4. Jay was not alone in finding circuit riding irksome. For Associate Justice William Cushing's complaints about "perpetual itineration," see Cushing to Iredell, Feb. 13, 1791, Cushing Papers, Massachusetts Historical Society.

NOTES

5. Alexander Hamilton to JJ, Nov. 13, 1790; JJ to Hamilton, Nov. 28, 1790 (draft), JP.

6. Hayburn's Case, 2 Dallas 408 (1792). See also note by Chief Justice Taney on U.S. *v.* Yale Todd (1794), 13 Howard 52 (1851); Charles Warren, *The Supreme Court in United States History* (Boston, Toronto, 1926), I:70 *et seq.*

7. Thomas Jefferson to Chief Justice Jay and Associate Justices, July 18, 1793; Chief Justice Jay and Associate Justices to President Washington, July 20, 1793; Chief Justice Jay and Associate Justices to President Washington, Aug. 8, 1793, all in *JPJ*, III:486–489.

8. Alexander Hamilton to JJ, Sept. 3, 1792, April 9, 1793, JP; JJ to Hamilton, Sept. 8, 1792, April 11, 1793, *ibid.*; drafts of Senate committee reports of Jan. 19 and March 1, 1791, Record Group 46, Senate 1B–B5 and 1B–B2, National Archives.

9. James Sullivan, *Observations upon the Government of the United States of America* (Boston, 1791), p. 41; Timothy Ford, *An Enquiry into the Constitutional Authority of the Supreme Federal Court over the Several States in Their Political Capacity* (Charleston, S.C., 1792).

10. Iredell to JJ, Jan. 17, 1792, James Iredell Papers, North Carolina State Department of Archives and History.

11. For a perpetuation of this error, see Warren, *Supreme Court,* I:93. Pickering's reports give no more facts about the case than Dallas. The writer is particularly indebted to his former student, Kemp Yarborough, whose detailed analysis, "Chisholm *v.* Georgia: A Study in American Constitutional History" (Unpubl. diss., Columbia University, 1963), has been drawn upon at numerous points in his treatment of the case.

12. The accounts were certified by three witnesses acquainted with Farquhar's handwriting, such certification having been taken before a district judge in South Carolina. Chisholm *v.* Georgia, Records, Supreme Court, U.S. Original Case Files; Federal Records Center, East Point, Ga., file papers in Chisholm *v.* Georgia.

13. Leonard White, *The Federalists, A Study in Administrative History* (New York, 1948), p. 170.

14. Chisholm *v.* Georgia, 2 Dallas 419, 421–427.

15. Aug. 5, 1793, Minutes of the Supreme Court of the United States, RG 267, National Archives (Reel 1 of microfilm edition); Feb. 14, 1794, *ibid.*

16. Aug. 5, 1794, *ibid.*

17. Henry Flanders, *The Lives and Times of the Chief Justices of the Supreme Court of the United States* (New York, 1875), II:33–35.

18. John D. Cushing, "A Revolutionary Conservative: The Pub-

lic Life of William Cushing, 1732–1810" (unpubl. diss., Clark University, 1960).

19. *Ibid.*

20. 2 Dallas 419, 451–452, 467–468.

21. "An Address to the Inhabitants of the Colonies," 1776, in R. G. Adams, ed., *Selected Political Essays of James Wilson* (New York, 1930), pp. 15–16.

22. Wilson, "Considerations on the Power to Incorporate the Bank of North America," Adams, *ibid.*, pp. 132–133.

23. Max Farrand, ed., *Records of the Federal Convention* (New Haven, 1911), I:132, 133, 141, 359, 482, 483.

24. *Ibid.*, I:405, 406.

25. *Ibid.*, I:322, 323.

26. Elliot, *Debates* II:491; J. D. Andrews, ed., *Works of James Wilson* (Chicago, 1896), II:153.

27. 2 Dallas 419, 457, 458, 464.

28. See Frank Monaghan, *John Jay* (New York, Indianapolis, 1935), p. 322; and Pellew, *John Jay*, pp. 282–284.

29. 2 Dallas 419, 471–479.

30. See H. T. Lefler and A. R. Newsome, *The History of a Southern State: North Carolina* (Chapel Hill, 1954), pp. 273, 274; Louise I. Trenholme, *The Ratification of the Federal Constitution in North Carolina* (New York, 1932), pp. 33, 44, 45.

31. W. Clark, ed., *State Records of North Carolina* (Winston, 1895–1906), XXI:v.

32. "Answer to Mr. Mason's Objections to the New Constitution Recommended by the Late Convention," in Paul L. Ford, ed., *Pamphlets on the Constitution of the United States* (Brooklyn, 1888), p. 343.

33. 2 Dallas 419, 430–436. See also Yarborough, "Chisholm *v.* Georgia," chap. 4.

34. 2 Dallas 419, 436–449.

35. Kentucky *v.* Dennison, 24 How. 66, 96 (Taney, C. J.) (U.S. 1860).

36. E. S. Corwin, *The Constitution and What It Means Today* (Princeton, 1940), p. 122.

37. Iredell Memoranda in Charles H. Johnson Collection, North Carolina State Archives, cited by Yarborough, "Chisholm *v.* Georgia."

38. Elliot, *Debates*, III:555–556.

39. Warren, *Supreme Court*, I:96; R. E. Cushman, *Leading Constitutional Decisions* (New York, 1950), p. 263.

40. H. V. Ames, ed., *State Documents on Federal Relations* (Philadelphia, 1906), pp. 7–11.

41. See also Opinion of Chief Justice Waite in New Hampshire v. Louisiana, 108 U.S. 76, 88 (1883); William Guthrie, "The Eleventh Amendment," *Columbia Law Review*, VIII:185 (March 1908).

42. *Annals of Congress*, 2nd Cong., 2nd Sess., pp. 651–652.

43. *Ibid.*, 3rd Cong., 1st Sess., pp. 25, 30, 31.

44. James Brown Scott, *Judicial Settlement of Controversies between States of the American Union* (Oxford, 1919), p. 62.

45. Quoted in G. J. McRee, ed., *The Life and Correspondence of James Iredell* (New York, 1857), II:348. See also Marshall in McCulloch v. Maryland, 4 Wheaton 316, 410 (1819).

46. Wheat. 264 (1821); T. M. Cooley, *The General Principles of Constitutional Law in the United States,* A. C. McLaughlin, ed. (Boston, 1898), p. 136.

47. New Hampshire v. Louisiana, 108 U.S. 76 (1883).

48. South Dakota v. North Carolina, 192 U.S. 286 (1904).

49. Carl Brent Swisher, *American Constitutional Development* (Boston, 1943), p. 88.

50. See Harry N. Scheiber, "The Condition of American Federalism: An Historian's View," A Study submitted by the Subcommittee on Intergovernmental Relations," 89th Cong., 2nd Sess. (Washington, 1966); but cf. Morton Grodzins, "Centralization and Decentralization," in R. A. Goldwin, ed., *A Nation of States* (Chicago, 1963). For a defense of Jay's position in Chisholm v. Georgia, see Kenneth B. Umbreit, *Our Eleven Chief Justices* (New York, 1938), pp. 41–45.

51. Chisholm v. Georgia, 2 Dallas 419, 476.

Chapter III. Jay, the Supreme Court, and the Supremacy of Treaties

1. See Jefferson's estimate in Boyd, *Papers of Thomas Jefferson*, X:27. Monroe put it somewhat higher (*ibid.*, VII:48). See also Emory G. Evans, "Planter Indebtedness and the Coming of the Revolution in Virginia," *William and Mary Quarterly*, 3rd Series, XIX:511–533 (1962). Cf. Thad W. Tate, "The Coming of the Revolution in Virginia," *ibid.*, pp. 323–343.

2. J. A. Ernst, "Genesis of the Currency Act of 1764," *William and Mary Quarterly*, 3rd Series, XXII:33–74 (1965).

3. Lawrence H. Gipson, "Virginia Planter Debts before the American Revolution," *Virginia Magazine of History and Biography*, LXIX:259–277 (1961).

4. George Mason to Patrick Henry, May 6, 1783, in William W. Henry, *Patrick Henry: Life, Correspondence and Speeches*

(New York, 1891), II:187. See also R. B. Morris, "Class Struggle and the American Revolution," *William and Mary Quarterly,* 3rd Series, XIX:24, 25 (1962); *The American Revolution Reconsidered* (New York, 1967), pp. 81–83.

5. Evans, "Planter Indebtedness," p. 531.

6. Dec. 18, 1776, *Journal of the House of Delegates,* U.S. Library of Congress, Records of the States of the U.S., Virginia (1 Microfilm, reel 3), pp. 138–139.

7. William Waller Hening, *Statutes of Virginia* (Richmond, 1821), IX:377–380.

8. See I. S. Harrell, *Loyalism in Virginia* (Durham, N.C., 1926), pp. 81–83.

9. Quotations in preceding three paragraphs in Morris, *The Peacemakers,* pp. 296, 318, 348, 350, 351, 361, 366, 367, 534.

10. JJ to Alexander McDougall, Dec. 23, 1775, March 27, April 27, 1776, McDougall Papers, N.Y. Historical Society; McDougall to JJ, April 16, 1776, JP.

11. April 13, 1787, *Journals of the Continental Congress,* XXXII:175–184. See also Bemis, "John Jay," in Bemis, *The American Secretaries of State,* I:228–230.

12. In Moncure D. Conway, *Omitted Chapters of History Disclosed in the Life and Papers of Edmund Randolph* (New York, London, 1889), p. 106.

13. Gaillard Hunt, ed., *The Writings of James Madison* (New York, 1900–1910), V:240–241.

14. *JPJ,* III:387–395.

15. Jay and District Judge Marchant at the June 1792 court term continued this case "by agreement" after invalidating the defendant's plea grounded in his petition to the General Assembly. Judgment in the amount of $19,987.55 was awarded the plaintiff in the November term, Wilson and Iredell substituting for Jay. U.S. Circuit Court, Rhode Island, 1790–1792 (Microfilm, reel 2).

16. *Providence Gazette,* June 23, 1792; Warren, *Supreme Court,* I:69.

17. James Iredell to Samuel Johnston, May 29, 1793, Hayes Papers, Edenton, N.C. (photostat in Jay Papers).

18. The opinion attributed in 2 Paine 688 to John Jay in Jones *v.* Walker is an erroneous attribution; the U.S. Circuit Court Order Book I, 1790–1795, for the District of Virginia, pp. 54–55, makes clear that Jay never sat in the case. This case was continued as Ware *v.* Walker. On May 27, 1797, with Iredell as the sole presiding judge, an opinion was handed down. The court issued judgment for the plaintiff on four pleas. The case, however, continued for at least two more years, through 1799. U.S. Circuit

Court, Order Book No. 2, 1795–1797, pp. 105, 221; U.S. Circuit Court, Record Book 5E, 1796–1797, pp. 287–302; U.S. Circuit Court, Order Book No. 3, 1797–1800, pp. 121, 204.

19. Ware v. Hylton had first come up on May 23, 1791, before Supreme Court Associate Justices Wilson and Iredell and District Judge Griffin and was then called Jones v. Hylton. It was argued in November 1791, before Judges Johnson and Griffin. Litigation continued for several years with Ware, executor for Jones, as the plaintiff. Subsequent quotations from U.S. Circuit Court Order Book I, 1790–1795, for the District of Virginia, pp. 7, 65–66, 141, 161, 162, 381, 386.

20. Henry, Life of Patrick Henry, II:473.

21. McRee, Life of Iredell, II:395.

22. June 15, 1793, General Advertiser, quoted by Warren, Supreme Court, I:145; McRee, Life of James Iredell, II:395. On the issue of Jay's dissent, cf. Barbara Bennett, "Settling the Revolutionary Debt Question: Ware v. Hylton and Jones v. Walker" (unpubl. diss., Columbia University, 1966).

23. Conway, Life of Randolph, p. 153.

24. Annals of Congress, 3rd Congress, 1st Sess., IV:94. See also Charles King, ed., The Life and Correspondence of Rufus King (New York, 1894–1900), I:525–527.

25. Connecticut Journal, Sept. 29, 1794.

26. Warren, Supreme Court, I:146. See the oration of William Henry Rawle, May 10, 1884, in The Orations of Chief Justice Waite and of William Henry Rawle on Chief Justice Marshall (Chicago, 1900), p. 36; A. J. Beveridge, The Life of John Marshall (Boston and New York, 1916), II:192–198. Wirt to Gilmer, Nov. 2, 1818, in John Pendleton Kennedy, ed., Wirt: Memoirs of the Life of William Wirt (Phiadelphia, 1849), II:82, 83.

27. 3 Dallas 199–285.

28. Journal of the House of Delegates, Nov. 1796, pp. 108, 127, 160, 194; Page v. Pendleton, Wythe, Chancery Reports 211–218 (1793).

29. Evans, "Planter Indebtedness," p. 518.

30. Virginia Reports Annotated 5–10 (2 Call 1–6) 2 Call 530. See also Hopkirk v. Bell, 3 Cranch 454–458 (1806).

31. JJ to Sarah Livingston Jay, April 15, 19, 1794, JP. See Henry Flanders, The Lives and Times of the Chief Justices of the Supreme Court of the United States (New York, 1875), I:404, for the erroneous attribution of these letters to 1790, and hence to Jay's acceptance of Washington's nomination to the Court.

32. The U.S. Government called upon Jay for advice on such questions before the mixed commission as the burden of proof of

solvency or insolvency and whether interest should be allowed for the wartime years; the last point was dealt with in Ware *v.* Hylton. Secretary of State Timothy Pickering to JJ, Dec. 13, 1797, JP. *American State Papers, Documents, Legislative and Executive of the Congress of the United States, Foreign Affairs* (Washington, 1832), II:382–428. See also S. F. Bemis, *Jay's Treaty, A Study in Commerce and Diplomacy* (New York, 1923), p. 318.

33. 3 Dallas 5 (U.S. 1794).

34. Warren, *Supreme Court,* I:117.

35. "Memorandum and Opinion in the Case of Ravara [*sic*] The Genoese Consul" (*c.*1795), McDougall Papers, N.Y. Historical Society. The trial of Joseph Ravara is reported in 2 Dallas 297; Francis Wharton, *State Trials* (Philadelphia, 1849), pp. 90–92.

36. John Jay to Washington, Sept. 23, 1791, Royal Archives, Windsor Castle; John Jay to Rufus King, Dec. 22, 1793, Rufus King Papers, N.Y. Historical Society. See Kathryn Turner, "Federalist Policy and the Judiciary Act of 1801," *William and Mary Quarterly,* XXII:5–7 (1965).

37. Taney, C. J., on Yale *v.* Todd, quoted in 13 How. 52 (1851).

38. Trial of Joseph Ravara, 2 Dall. 297 (1793–1794); Wharton, *State Trials,* pp. 90–92. The Jay doctrine is criticized in George Van Santvoord, *Sketches of the Lives and Judicial Services of the Chief-Justices of the Supreme Court of the United States* (New York, 1854), pp. 55–60, and in C. G. Haines, *The Role of the Supreme Court in American Government and Politics, 1789–1835* (New York, 1960), pp. 125–128, 306–308.

39. U.S. *v.* Hudson, 7 Cranch 32 (1812); see also Leonard W. Levy, *Legacy of Suppression* (Cambridge, Mass., 1960), pp. 239–241.

40. Swift *v.* Tyson, 16 Pet. 1 (1842); Erie Railroad Co. *v.* Tompkins, 304 U.S. 64 (1938).

41. Jay's charge to the jury in Georgia *v.* Brailsford, 2 Dall. 403, 415 (1794). See Flanders, *Chief Justices,* pp. 392–393, where Jay's statement of the extent of the jury's powers is dismissed as "clearly erroneous." Cf. Galloway *v.* United States, 319 U.S. 389, 399 (1943); Thayer, *On Evidence* (1898 ed.), p. 254.

CASES CITED